☆ RETURN OF THE BIG FIVE ☆

PLAYS BY HRANT ALIANAK

INTERVIEW BY URJO KAREDA

CONNIE BRISSENDEN
EDITOR
FINEGLOW

Cover design/Titles by E.Honour Dewart. Interior
design by Connie Brissenden. Typed with the
assistance of Frances Dvorchik.

Printed by the Hunter Rose Company for Fineglow
Plays, January 1975.

ISBN 0-9690496-1-7

Fineglow Plays
c/o The Playwrights Co-op
344 Dupont Street
Toronto M5R 1V9
Ontario

TO MY PARENTS

CONTENTS

INTERVIEW

URJO KAREDA and HRANT ALIANAK

KAREDA

How would you define the word "theatrical?"

ALIANAK

Everything is potentially theatrical, all of life. But for me, true theatricality refers to something bigger than life... on the scale of John Wayne or Jerry Lewis. Basically, it's fantasy presented in a realistic way. Theatre should lift you out of your real life situation and make you imagine that you're somewhere else. "Kitchen-sink" drama is too ordinary; it doesn't impress me.

KAREDA

Why are you drawn to theatre as opposed, say, to film?

ALIANAK

But I'm not really. I was never interested in theatre, I have always been more fascinated by movies, probably because I was brought up on them.

KAREDA

What films do you enjoy most?

ALIANAK

Films where you don't have to think. I like the James Bond flicks. The Poseidon Adventure, I liked that very much. I was just glued to the screen. You know these movies are pedestrian, but who cares? You're having the time of your life. I feel very comfortable watching a movie, very relaxed. If I have to cry, I cry. Laugh, I laugh.

Theatre is so severe compared to movies. There are so many rules "up there," onstage. And in the audience, you have to sit differently, react differently as well. Why?

KAREDA

Yes, theatre can be boring, I agree. It's so regimented, with so many rules. You have to arrive at a certain time, sit in a certain place, go home at a certain time...

ALIANAK

...and you can't boo and cheer like you can in movies. Because of the severity, theatre loses so much. I'd rather go to a film anyday. There are so many things going for movies. They're phony, but you grow to like that. And expect it.

KAREDA

Do movies provide a strong visual character for your plays? So many people remember them as pictures, at least I do anyway. Almost in a frame.

ALIANAK

Film will always be a major influence in my work. I strive for the same kind of continuity. Unfortunately you can't have close-ups and zoom shots in theatre. So, obviously, sets and lighting have to play an important part. And yet, interestingly enough, the sets for my plays in most cases have been minimal. Most of them have been done on next to bare stages with the exception of BRANDY, a beautiful set. It was more elaborate but still minimal. And, oh yes, NOAH'S KIOSK... but, well, what can I say about that?

KAREDA

What can you say? Do you think NOAH'S KIOSK was a failure?

ALIANAK

Yes.

KAREDA
Why do you think it failed?

ALIANAK
A lot of reasons. The production never got off
the ground for one thing...there were a number
of technical details that I'd planned to use that
never happened. I mean, the set was still being
painted on opening night!

But mainly, I have to admit, the biggest fault
was the script. It just wasn't ready. I fooled
myself into thinking it was even when it was
obviously not working. There were so many ideas
in my head, I wanted to try them all out. What
was in my head and what happened onstage were
two completely different things. Like the egg
falling sequence, for example. That was so stupid.
I'd read so many comic books, I thought that when
the egg was dropped on the actor's head, it
would stay there in the shape of a fried egg. How
I thought this I don't know now. When we tried
it, the yolk, of course, didn't stay in one place
...it dribbled all over him. But I was working
with that image all the time, thinking it would
be strong enough to sustain action for five
minutes. Hah! Everything went wrong.

I wish it had been my money put out for the
production. I would have simply said, "Sorry,
it's not opening." But it wasn't, so on it went.

KAREDA
Would you classify yourself as an experimental
writer?

ALIANAK

My writing, at least what's been seen at this
point, tends to be innovative I guess. I don't
like the word "experimental." I've chosen to
write my kind of plays because I can't express
myself in a realistic way. Maybe someday?

My favorite writers are Eugene O'Neil, Arthur
Miller, Chekhov, Neil Simon. I particularly like
Neil Simon, I've read or seen every one of his
plays.

KAREDA

What kind of theatre are you trying to write?

ALIANAK

What I'm aiming for is entertainment on The
Poseidon Adventure level. Plays that will appeal
to everybody. I don't want to insult my audience's intelligence, but I try to tone down the
intellectual level until it's very basic and can
be enjoyed by everyone.

I've only been in this business for two years. My
outlook has been, well, "artsy-craftsy" I suppose.
Although I enjoy my kind of theatre and will
defend it to the end, it's not the only kind of
theatre I believe in.

KAREDA

You say you liked The Poseidon Adventure because
it was exciting, but in NOAH'S KIOSK I was bored
because nothing was happening. Do you feel the

same way, or do you think inaction can be
exciting?

        ALIANAK
No, I was bored too. NOAH'S KIOSK was a failure.
I intended to have so much action that you
wouldn't be able to catch your breath...like
BRANDY...but it didn't happen that way.

        KAREDA
How do you start with a play like BRANDY? Is
there a long planning process? Or do you write
immediately, instinctively?

        ALIANAK
I had no concrete ideas for BRANDY. In this
particular case I had committed myself to doing
a play for Paul Thompson, any play, and I
needed one fast, in two weeks. So home I went,
to my files. There were about six unfinished
plays lying around, and I experimented with them.
I found four characters. Then I discovered the
sequence with the blonde running around with the
nitroglycerine but it was written in another
style, so I had to fix it up. The scene with
the brunette and the blond was first written for
a man and the blonde but when I saw the brunette
didn't have too much to do, I made the necessary
changes...

The Tarzan sequence just popped into my head.
All these ridiculous ideas just popped into my
head. A Volkswagon? Across the desert? It was
so stupid that I began to like it.

The original ending of BRANDY was terrible. I
brought in the new ending a couple of days before
the opening. It came from some dialogue I had
written for a potential gangster story.

Of course, this way I lose a lot of plays! I make
one play and in the process I destroy six others.

At first, I didn't exactly know what was going on.
I just threw everything together. Then came the
cutting, and I started to make' some sense.

            KAREDA
Do your actors sometimes add dialogue or business
to your plays in rehearsals which you later
incorporate into your scenario?

            ALIANAK
All the time. I'm very ruthless with my scripts.
If there's a better suggestion, I'll use it. I'm
always open to change.

            KAREDA
Are you astounded when people analyse or articulate
what your plays are about?

            ALIANAK
No, not at all. When I write them, I admit, it's
all very subconscious. I don't know why I'm
writing certain things. Why Tarzan? Why Volkswagon? I suppose it's primarily because of
influences in my childhood...I did drive a Volkswagon across the desert. I did like Tarzan movies.

But in the end, analysis is surely called for.
BRANDY is a fairly complex play, I think it has
a lot to say.

In a way, I wait for the reviews to come out so
they can tell me what my play is all about!

                    KAREDA
Do you think audiences have to bring methods of
perceiving to your plays which are out of the
ordinary? Do they have to reach back to a way of
looking at plays that they may not be used to?
Either more sophisticated, or less?

                    ALIANAK
Less sophisticated perhaps. I'm not trying to
impress anyone, I'm not after creating new forms.
My style developed subconsciously. I didn't sit
down and try to figure it out. My plays are a
little unusual perhaps but basically all my
stories are old stories. They've been told 20,000
times before. Rather than tell them in the same
way, I've tried to tell them in a new way.

                    KAREDA
Originally CHRISTMAS was staged as a play without
words, yet in the script version you've added
dialogue. Don't you think that people will be
tempted to perform the dialogue?

                    ALIANAK
They might, but they shouldn't. The only reason

I wrote it with dialogue was because it was the
only way I could write it. I'd been stalled with
the script for six months because I couldn't find
a written style for it.

                    KAREDA
Why don't you use dialogue in the production?

                    ALIANAK
It's not really necessary. It's redundant. The
story can be told without it, so why use it?
Without the dialogue the play is clean, neat, told
in the universal language.

I asked my actors to memorize the dialogue and say
it very silently. If I'd only included stage
directions, they might have gone into mime and I
didn't want that. The characters are supposed to
be speaking normally, only we can't hear them.

                    KAREDA
Are you slightly suspicious of dialogue? Or the
necessity for dialogue?

                    ALIANAK
In this play? Or generally?

                    KAREDA
Generally.

                    ALIANAK
I was, but not anymore. Two years ago, I was

very bad at writing dialogue. So I got around
it in other ways. Using little tricks, like in
MATHEMATICS and WESTERN, and in TANTRUMS as well.
In BRANDY I was able to write dialogue, even
though it was all over the place at first. Since
then I've written several dialogue plays and it's
coming easier to me now.

                    KAREDA
Can you achieve complexity of character without
dialogue? You could tell <u>Three Sisters</u> in ten
minutes...

                    ALIANAK
Of course. I'm not comparing myself to Chekhov
or Shaw...they were writing language, not merely
dialogue.

                    KAREDA
But are you interested in complex characters? Or
are you more interested in patterns?

                    ALIANAK
In the past I worked more with patterns. But I'm
changing. I think more about characterization
nowadays. The Christmas tree in CHRISTMAS is
probably the most detailed character I've created.
Most of my characters are one-dimensional. Sometimes on purpose, sometimes they just come out
that way.

                    KAREDA
For audiences, in some ways, dialogue is a kind

of comfort. It makes judgements for them, it
tells a certain amount. By removing it from
them, you make them responsible for putting the
story together in their heads. I think you
require much freer responses to your plays.

ALIANAK
The funny thing is that kids like my plays very
much. They respond quickly to them. They loved
CHRISTMAS. And NOAH'S KIOSK, only kids liked
that.

KAREDA
What happens to people between the time when
they're kids and love a play like NOAH'S KIOSK
and the time they're adults and can't enjoy it
the same way? Why can't we always look at plays
the way a child looks at them?

ALIANAK
I'm not sure...I guess we pile up too many
defences. In NOAH'S KIOSK, for example, the
last scene was supposed to be tender, touching.
But people sneered at it. At a dress rehearsal,
one woman cried out, "Oh, come on." She was
fighting against it. Audiences can't accept a
tear-jerker and let it go at that. Perhaps with
CHRISTMAS I've been able to soften up my
audience. There were a lot of wet eyes at the
end of that play.

That's all I'm really interested in, all kinds
of emotional responses whether they're tears or

laughter, cheering or booing. Simple reactions
make me feel more fulfilled as a playwright. I
prefer these responses to the intellectual ones.

KAREDA
Do you think BRANDY requires an intellectual
analysis?

ALIANAK
Yes, BRANDY is different. But in a way, not.
There were a lot of kids in the audience for it
as well and they seemed to understand it better
than the adults did. The play was so cartoonish
they forgot about the dialogue completely. They
let it pass by and enjoyed the cartoon aspects,
like for instance, a punch on the nose, that sort
of thing. Which I'm more interested in anyway.
I spend more time on a punch on the nose than I
do on dialogue. In a way, I work against my
script, cheating a little. The audience is intent
on the dialogue when actually I consider the real
stuff is going on in that simple punch.

KAREDA
I would have thought that in BRANDY, the dialogue
is extremely well-planned. I'd say that BRANDY
is clear evidence that you can write dialogue.

ALIANAK
But again, I sabotaged the script by having the
actors rattle it off as fast as they could. Somebody said to me, "I wanted to laugh, there were
jokes there, but I didn't have time. Everything

was going so fast. I had to be constantly alert
with it." Well, that's true, but if the play
had been done slowly, I don't think it would
have been very effective.

KAREDA

Let's say somebody wants to direct BRANDY in
Yellowknife and they don't have any idea of how
you originally staged it against the dialogue.
Are you quite prepared to have a different play
emerge from their production?

ALIANAK

No, I hate the idea. I don't think I'd want to
see any productions of my plays directed by
someone else...if someone wants to do one in some
distant place, fine. I just won't go and see it.
It's inevitably going to be a different play. No
matter how I try I won't be able to explain it
to another director.

KAREDA

What about TANTRUMS? Did you write it to direct
it?

ALIANAK

No. I happened to act in a play that Louis Del
Grande did and I mentioned to him that I had a
script. He read it, liked it, and did it. It
was impossible for me to direct it, even if I'd
wanted to. Nobody was going to give me a chance,
no-one knew me. I was very fortunate in getting

a good response to that production, it opened
doors for me. People were very anxious to see
my plays after that, but I wanted to direct them
myself. I had to say no to other directors. In
the end, I chose a difficult route. No-one
would let me direct, so I wrote short plays to
experiment with, to be able to say, "Look, I can
direct, let me do it myself."

            KAREDA
What do you look for in plays by other writers?
What makes them plays you'd like to direct?

            ALIANAK
Basically, what I look for in a script is a good
evening's entertainment. That's my guideline.

            KAREDA
You've said that the first professional theatre
you'd ever seen was <u>The Sound of Music</u>. Did that
production have any effect on you?

            ALIANAK
Oh, I loved it. I was fascinated by the play. It
was so innocent, so nice, and the music was
excellent. I love musicals. But it didn't
really influence me...it just happened to be the
first play I ever saw.

            KAREDA
What role does music take when you write your
plays? Is it very influential?

ALIANAK

Yes, very. One thing I regret is not being
able to write music. I have music in every
one of my plays, it's an excellent mood setter.
CHRISTMAS is dead without music. All of my
plays need music.

That's the fault with a lot of theatre I see.
No music. Perhaps I feel this way because I
was brought up on the movies and I keep searching
for that musical background.

KAREDA

What sort of feelings do you have about inanimate
objects? Are you fascinated by them? Is this
an influence of cartoons?

ALIANAK

It's probably because of cartoons. Though I
think I'm more fascinated by animals than by
inanimate objects. I watch Bugs Bunny and
Sylvester all the time. I enjoy the way these
animals have been made into humans. They're
the kind of characters I look for. Extravagant
and innocent.

KAREDA

Half your plays are sentimental- in the good
sense- the other half are cynical. Do you
think the two are reconcilable? Are you a
schizophrenic, Mr Alianak?

ALIANAK

My earlier plays are cynical. But after I wrote
TANTRUMS, particularly Tantrum Four, what more
could I say? I felt I'd just be repeating myself
if I stayed with this type of play. That was the
ultimate statement I could make about terror and
depression. I knew that I either had to get out
of theatre or go somewhere else in my writing.
So I went to sadness. I'm still saying the same
thing really, but in a different way.

When I wrote TANTRUMS, I hated sentimentality. I
made a conscious effort to write against it. With
THE VIOLINIST AND THE FLOWER GIRL, which I wrote
around that time, and which is a very sentimental
play, I made fun of it. Then, little by little,
I asked myself, "Why am I making fun of this?"

Sentimentality is not in vogue in theatre today.
I don't care. I'm doing it and I like it. Maybe
I even like the fact that no-one else is doing it.

I saw a Charlie Chaplin movie recently. What can
I say? The man is a genius and his movies reek
of sentimentality. And the audience's reactions
were honest. That's why I'm writing sentimental
plays now. I love that kind of reaction and I
want to get it out of my audiences.

THE END

This play is about one day
(any day)
in the life
of a normal
fairly well-to-do
married
childless
couple
(any couple).

MATHEMATICS is divided into
six scenes.

There is a ten second pause
between each scene,
before the first scene,
and after the last scene.

There are five objects in
every scene.

There is a five second pause
between every object
in every scene.

The defined objects are to be
thrown onstage
but the throwers themselves
should not be visible.

The stage should be divided
into six areas.

Each scene should have a
clearly defined and
separate stage area.

Each object should be clearly visible, after being
thrown onstage.

The entire length of the
play should have a musical
accompaniment.

The musical accompaniment
should have a constant and
methodical beat.

The exact duration of this
play is 190 seconds,
or, three minutes and ten
seconds.

SCENE ONE

A duster.....a dust-pan.....
a pail.....a bottle of
detergent.....a bottle of
coffee

SCENE TWO

A brief-case.....an umbrella
.....a raincoat.....a hat.....
a bunch of flowers

SCENE THREE

A glass.....a plate.....a
spoon.....a bag of spaghetti
.....a roll of toilet paper

SCENE FOUR

A newspaper.....a shoe.....a
TV GUIDE.....a beer can.....
a bag of potato chips

SCENE FIVE

A dress.....a pair of trousers
.....a sock.....a brassiere
.....a toothbrush

SCENE SIX

A pillow.....a copy of PLAYBOY
magazine.....a pair of pyjama
bottoms.....a pack of cigarettes
.....an alarm clock

THE END

TANTRUMS

TANTRUM ONE

One neutral abstract set for all
four TANTRUMS, with perhaps an
obstacle in the background. White
on black.

A siren. Long and loud.

A countdown. On tape; perhaps
9978 to 9954.

All throughout TANTRUM ONE, jarring,
shattering, clattering, tinkling,
clanking music. Loud, insistent and
irritating. It stops momentarily
for the actors to speak their given
lines, then comes up even louder.

Lights.

A table, three chairs and a wheelchair.

PAPA, in wheelchair and neck-brace.
He smokes a pipe.

MAMA, pretty, a model housewife. She
knits.

SONNY. He reads a heavy book.

All are dressed in neutral black.

In an obscure corner, a LITTLE GIRL.
Sitting quite still and immobile, on
the floor, back to audience. She
remains immobile until the end. She
is dressed in white.

Long pause.

The family smiles a lot.

PAPA smiles at MAMA.
MAMA smiles back.
PAPA smiles at SONNY.
SONNY smiles back.
PAPA and SONNY smile at MAMA.
MAMA smiles back.

This ritual is repeated four times,
very slowly.

Suddenly they are confronted by the
stunning presence of a stranger,
evaporated from nowhere, now standing somewhere behind the table,
next to MAMA.

He is black.
He is in black.
He is GASPARD.

They all stare at him silently.

Long pause.

MAMA: (Polite) Do you do this often? I mean
barge into people's homes unannounced?

GASPARD: (Polite) You had advertised for help.

(Pause. Music continues)

MAMA: (Still polite) I'm so sorry. The position
has been taken!

GASPARD: (Also polite) I can help you!

(Inaudible conversation between MAMA,
PAPA and GASPARD, always polite.
Music continues)

37

PAPA: We can't afford to pay you much though!

GASPARD: Oh, that's quite all right! Incidentally, I have unpacked my bags in one of your rooms!

>(More inaudible conversation between
>the three, politeness now being some-
>what strained. Music continues)

PAPA: You're quite welcome to the guest room!

GASPARD: (Pleasant) Oh, it's your room I've moved into!

>(More inaudible conversation.
>Politeness gone. Music continues)

GASPARD: (To MAMA) May I have something to eat please? I'm rather hungry!

MAMA: (Frosty) In the kitchen.

>(Music continues. GASPARD stares at
>her piercingly but politely, then
>slowly pulls a chair and sits at the
>table)

GASPARD: I'm very hungry!

>(Music continues. A pregnant pause,
>then MAMA stomps out to the kitchen.

>BLACKOUT

Music continues.

>LIGHTS

>MAMA is back at table. There is a tray
>of food near GASPARD.

There is a long pause.

GASPARD stares fixedly at MAMA.
Finally, MAMA gets up, seething with
rage, places knife, fork, glass and
plate in front of him, and sits again.

Another long pause.

GASPARD still stares at her fixedly.
MAMA is now a furiously controlled
nervous mess. She gets up again and
serves him his food. She is about to
place the bottle of wine in front of
him, but changes her mind and sarcas-
tically pours it for him. She sits.
They now all watch the content
GASPARD eat, even SONNY.

Music continues, but not as loud as
before. This goes on for two whole
minutes.

BLACKOUT

Music continues louder.

LIGHTS

PAPA smoking pipe meditatively.

SONNY immersed in heavy book.

MAMA knitting, furious and nervous.

GASPARD, now at head of table, reading a newspaper.

This goes on for one minute.

Finally GASPARD puts down the paper,
gets up, stretches and stares intently
at MAMA)

GASPARD: Good night.

MAMA: Good night.

PAPA: Good night, Mr Gaspard.

(Pause)

GASPARD: Good night.

MAMA: Good night.

PAPA: Good night, Mr Gaspard.

(Pause)

GASPARD: Good night.

MAMA: Good night.

PAPA: Good night, Mr Gaspard.

(Pause)

GASPARD: Good night.

MAMA: Good night.

PAPA: Good night, Mr Gaspard.

(Pause. MAMA is now shocked with the
final dawning of truth)

GASPARD: Good night.

MAMA: Good night.

PAPA: Good night, Mr Gaspard.

(Pause. Extremely intense, screaming
at each other now)

GASPARD: Good night.

MAMA: Good night.

PAPA: Good night, Mr Gaspard.

GASPARD: Good night.

MAMA: Good night.

PAPA: Good night, Mr Gaspard.

GASPARD: Good night.

MAMA: Good night.

PAPA: Good night, Mr Gaspard.

       (Pause.

       Music continues.

       MAMA now rises tearfully, exchanging
       helpless glances with PAPA. SONNY
       lunges savagely at GASPARD with a
       knife. GASPARD easily subdues him.
       He looks at him blankly, but without
       any hatred. He exits to the bedroom,
       beckoning MAMA after him, who follows
       helplessly. PAPA starts crying
       bitterly. SONNY comforts him. They
       exchange some inaudible conversation,
       then SONNY resignedly goes back to
       his book, and PAPA mournfully to his
       pipe.

               BLACKOUT

       Music continues.

               LIGHTS

PAPA and SONNY have disappeared. The
front of the stage is lit dimly. The
rest is plunged in darkness.

GASPARD and MAMA stand facing each
other. MAMA is naked. She is
bitter. GASPARD is politely blank.
He is naked from the waist up. MAMA
is passive, but still bitter. GASPARD
continues staring at her. MAMA
finally falls to her knees.

At this point the LITTLE GIRL slowly
turns around revealing a small red
ball in her lap. She stares at
GASPARD who still maintains his blank
look, then gently rolls the ball
towards him.

BLACKOUT

A siren. Long and loud.

A countdown; on tape; perhaps 5438
to 5382 or for the duration of
scene change)

TANTRUM TWO

In the background, posters of films
from the romantic thirties.

Announced by some pompous music, the
two USHERS enter, stand facing each
other in the background, and all
throughout, read titles of films to
each other, the text of which is
provided at the end of TANTRUM TWO.

Street sounds are heard. Crowds,
cars, etc.

Slowly these sounds seem to be making
a sort of jangling music. A rhythmical
alteration of the music, in TANTRUM
ONE, is heard. Again it's a clanking
melange of shrill sounds.

Two MEN enter, dressed in the thirties
period, with straw hats. They belong
to the glorious cinema crowd. They
are naive and ecstatic.

Two WOMEN enter, same period dress,
faded and summery. They are WOMEN
of the streets and are heavily painted.
They are all-knowing and hard.

The manner of walking of these two
couples is theatrically expansive
and arrogantly ˙exaggerated.

Their subsequent encounters are
pointedly dangerous and sadistically
violent.

The two parties see each other.

The MEN comment on the WOMEN. They
are extremely eager to prove their
sexual prowess. They happily agree
to approach the WOMEN.

They announce themselves victoriously.

The WOMEN don't take this too kindly
and merely scorn them derisively.

The conversation between the two
parties is loud and cool. The words
pertain to an unintelligible non-
existent language.

The WOMEN move away.

The MEN pursue them.

Another conversation in gibberish.
Very loud and impolite. No known
words are however heard.

The WOMEN move away.

The MEN are now determined.

They approach them once more.

The conversation is now extremely
loud and indignant.

The WOMEN move away.

The MEN are furious.

They approach them.

The conversation is now a mixture of
unpleasant shrieks, with gesticulating
canes and purses.

One of the MEN suddenly takes out a
roll of money and shows it to the
WOMEN.

The conversation stops.

The music continues.

The MEN wait while the WOMEN take an
interminable time counting the money.

They are satisfied. They smile.
They wink their eyes.

One of the WOMEN hands the money to
her companion, and with seductive
leers and grotesque waving of hips
leads the MAN who handed over the
money somewhere behind the obstacle
in the background.

The other MAN stands guard in front
in case of intruders.

The other WOMAN sits somewhere and
smokes a cigarette, very nonchalant.

They avoid eye contact.

The posters are spotlighted. Maurice
Chevalier. Jeanette MacDonald. Mary
Pickford. Nelson Eddy. Joan Craw-
ford. Mae West. Etc.

Crowd noises rise up again.

The MAN guarding is extremely uneasy.

A wild cacophony of laughter is heard.

The MAN is very embarrassed.

He impatiently waits for the two to come out.

The WOMAN finally comes out. She is rather merry as she exchanges a few pleasantries with her friend who hands her the money.

The MAN comes out. He seems to be in a daze. He is downcast and shamefaced. He is about to exit.

His companion tries to hold him back for an explanation, but he fiercely pulls away and disappears.

The laughter is still there, even louder.

The other MAN decides to exit as well, but the other WOMAN quickly steps up and hypnotically pulls him along behind the obstacle.

Again the posters are spotlighted.

The other WOMAN nonchalantly applies some make-up to her face.

The laughter stops.

Only the music is heard.

The WOMAN comes out, joins her friend and they exit happily.

The MAN does not come out.

The obstacle is lit and behind it is discerned the prostrate body of the MAN.

> A LITTLE GIRL is sitting beside him,
> staring out at the audience. She
> does not have her red ball.

BLACKOUT

> A siren. Long and loud.
>
> A countdown: on tape, perhaps 1654
> to 1592 or for the duration of the
> scene change.
>
> The titles should be read one at a
> time alternately by the MALE and
> FEMALE USHERS.

MALE USHER: Red Sun.
FEMALE USHER: At Home.
MALE: First Love.
FEMALE: High Flight.
MALE: Night People.
FEMALE: Out West.
MALE: Nudist Paradise.
FEMALE: Party Girl.
MALE: Night Heat.
FEMALE: Great Guns.
MALE: Dark Victory.
FEMALE: Girl's Town.
MALE: Circus World.
FEMALE: Brotherly Love.
MALE: Odd Obsession.
MALE: Crooks Anonymous.
FEMALE: Flat Top.
MALE: Man Trap.
FEMALE: Flood Tide.
MALE: Magic Boy.
FEMALE: Fury River.
MALE: Raw Edge.
FEMALE: Toy Tiger.
MALE: Water Birds.
FEMALE: Red Mountain.

MALE: Habeas Corpus.
FEMALE: Hidden Fortress.
MALE: Desert Hell.
FEMALE: Town Tamer.
MALE: Short Kilts.
FEMALE: Top Gun.
MALE: Stolen Hours.
FEMALE: Hello Sister.
MALE: Paradise Lost.
FEMALE: Young Fury.
MALE: Wrong Again.
FEMALE: Virgin Island.
MALE: Family Diary.
FEMALE: Time Limit.
MALE: Seven Thunders.
FEMALE: Flaming Star.
MALE: Two Loves.
FEMALE: Baby Doll.
MALE: Summer Magic.
FEMALE: Yellow Sky.
MALE: Bitter Rice.
FEMALE: Damn Citizen.
MALE: White Feather.
FEMALE: Autumn Leaves.
MALE: Battle Cry.
FEMALE: Little Women.
MALE: Ride Lonesome.
FEMALE: Something Big.
MALE: Hard Contract.
FEMALE: Sweet Ecstasy.
MALE: Loving You.
FEMALE: Silent Enemy.
MALE: Time Lock.
FEMALE: White Tower.
MALE: Naked Street.
FEMALE: Blowing Wild.
MALE: Secret People.
FEMALE: Fool's Paradise.
MALE: Sea Devils.
FEMALE: Iron Man.
MALE: Scarlet Angel.
FEMALE: Hornet's Nest.

MALE: Danger Route.
FEMALE: Ship Ahoy.
MALE: Step Lively.
FEMALE: Brute Force.
MALE: Bright Leaf.
FEMALE: City Streets.
MALE: Lilac Time.
FEMALE: Wild River.
MALE: Chain Lightning.
FEMALE: Stand In.
MALE: Dead Reckoning.
FEMALE: Crime School.
MALE: Black Legion.
FEMALE: Perfect Strangers.
MALE: Bad Boy.
FEMALE: Thunder Rock.
MALE: Black Magic.
FEMALE: Hot Spell.
MALE: Secret Ceremony.
FEMALE: Pocket Money.
MALE: Play Dirty.
FEMALE: Tall Story.
MALE: Shock Corridor.
FEMALE: That Woman.
MALE: To Love.
FEMALE: Love Nest.
MALE: One Room.
FEMALE: Penny Paradise.
MALE: Raw Deal.
FEMALE: Rainbow Dance.
MALE: Pure Love.
FEMALE: Four Sons.
MALE: Black Gravel.
FEMALE: Brief City.
MALE: Man Crazy.
FEMALE: Nobody's Darling.
MALE: Side Street.
FEMALE: New Snow.
MALE: Sudden Fear.
FEMALE: White Angel.
MALE: Young People.
FEMALE: One Week.

MALE: Love Affair.
FEMALE: In Between.
MALE: Girl Shy.
FEMALE: Forever Female.
MALE: The Most Beautiful Woman In The World.
FEMALE: The Bottom of the Bottle.
MALE: A Cold Wind in August.
FEMALE: The Wild and the Willing.
MALE: All the Brothers Were Valiant.
FEMALE: Indiscretion of an American Wife.
MALE: The Man Who Knew Too Much.
FEMALE: Love is a Many Splendoured Thing.
MALE: How to Save a Marriage and Ruin Your Life.
FEMALE: Last of the Mobile Hot Shots.
MALE: Here We Go Round the Mulberry Bush.
FEMALE: All the Fine Young Cannibals.
MALE: What Did You Do In The War, Daddy?
FEMALE: Don't Raise the Bridge, Lower the River.
MALE: The Greatest Story Ever Told.
FEMALE: The Secret of Convict Lake.
MALE: Heaven With a Barbed Wire Fence.
FEMALE: On the Way to the Crusades.
MALE: The Man Who Had Power Over Women.
FEMALE: Has Anybody Seen My Gal?
MALE: Take Me Out to the Ball Game.
FEMALE: Once you Kiss a Stranger.
MALE: 'Til the Clouds Roll By.
FEMALE: You Can't Get Away With Murder.
MALE: Thank Your Lucky Stars.
FEMALE: Start the Revolution Without Me.
MALE: Love is Where you Find it.
FEMALE: The Girl who had Everything.
MALE: The Day the Earth Stood Still.
FEMALE: Let No Man Write My Epitaph.
MALE: You Can't Take it with You.
FEMALE: Once Upon a Honeymoon.
MALE: Never the Twain Shall Meet.
FEMALE: People Meet and Sweet Music Fills the Heart.
MALE: Our Vines Have Tender Grapes.
FEMALE: A Report on the Party and the Guests.
MALE: The Record of a Tenement Gentleman.

FEMALE: The Story of the Last Chrysanthemums.
MALE: Love Among the Millionaires.
FEMALE: A Man and his Dog Out For Air.
MALE: How Grandpa Changed 'til Nothing was Left.
FEMALE: Love is Shared Like Sweets.
MALE: Love Me and the World is Mine.
FEMALE: The Woman who Touched the Legs.
MALE: When a Woman Ascends the Stairs.
FEMALE: The Plain Man's Guide to Advertising.
MALE: When Love Comes to the Village.
FEMALE: There Lived an Old Man and an Old Woman.
MALE: They Knew What They Wanted.
FEMALE: Sunday Dinner for a Soldier.
MALE: The Real End of the Great War.
FEMALE: On the Night of the Fire.
MALE: A Big Hand For the Little Lady.
FEMALE: Days of Thrills and Laughter.
MALE: Four Million Miles a Week.
FEMALE: Inauguration of the Pleasure Dome.
MALE: The Little Shepherd of Kingdom Come.
FEMALE: The Man Who Wanted to Live Forever.
MALE: The Happiest Days of Your Life.
FEMALE: A Time to Love and a Time to Die.
MALE: Shadows of our Forgotten Ancestors.
FEMALE: Slave Trades in the World Today.
MALE: The Man Who Could Work Miracles.
FEMALE: Little Pearls From the Bottom.
MALE: I'd Climb the Highest Mountain.
FEMALE: Days and Nights in the Forest.
MALE: A Little Phantasy on a 19th Century
Painting.
FEMALE: I Know Where I'm Going.
MALE: Shoot Loud, Louder... I don't Understand.
FEMALE: Doctor, You've got to be Kidding.
MALE: The Secret Life of an American Wife.
FEMALE: The Story of a Three Day Pass.
MALE: Decline and Fall of a Birdwatcher.
FEMALE: The Girl Who Couldn't Say No.
MALE: Today We Kill, Tomorrow We Die.
FEMALE: Work is a Four Letter Word.
MALE: Adam and Eve.
FEMALE: John and Mary.

MALE: Solomon and Sheba.
FEMALE: Samson and Delilah.
MALE: Romeo and Juliet.
FEMALE: Caesar and Cleopatra.
MALE: Bonnie and Clyde.
FEMALE: Sodom and Gommorah.
MALE: David and Bathsheba.
FEMALE: Minnie and Moscowitz.
MALE: Antoine and Antoinette.
FEMALE: Edouard and Caroline.
MALE: Jules and Jim.
FEMALE: Nicholas and Alexandra.
MALE: Peter and Pavla.
FEMALE: Hugo and Josephine.
MALE: Minin and Pozharsky.
FEMALE: Frankie and Johnny.
MALE: Romanoff and Juliet.
FEMALE: Harold and Maud.
MALE: Tillie and Gus.
FEMALE: Alise and Chloe.
MALE: David and Goliath.
FEMALE: Romulus and Remus.
MALE: Therese and Isabelle.
FEMALE: Orazi and Curiazi.
MALE: Salt and Pepper.
FEMALE: Von Richthofen and Brown.
MALE: Little Fauss and Big Halsey.
FEMALE: Butch Cassidy and the Sundance Kid.
MALE: The Cat and the Canary.
FEMALE: The Prince and the Pauper.
MALE: The Barbarian and the Giesha.
FEMALE: The Cowboy and the Lady.
MALE: The Bullfighter and the Lady.
FEMALE: The Beauty and the Beast.
MALE: A Man and a Woman.
FEMALE: King and Country.
MALE: Lady and the Tramp.
FEMALE: Me and the Colonel.
MALE: My Love and I.
FEMALE: The Owl and the Pussycat.
MALE: The Lady and the Pirate.
FEMALE: The Baby and the Battleship.

MALE: Orange and Blue.
FEMALE: The Prince and the Showgirl.
MALE: Snow White and the Seven Dwarfs.
FEMALE: Snow White and the Three Stooges.
MALE: The Virgin and the Gypsy.
FEMALE: David and Lisa.
MALE: Susan and God.
FEMALE: The Princess and the Pirate.
MALE: Mr. and Mrs. Smith.
FEMALE: Mr. and Mrs. Swordplay.
MALE: Mr. Peabody and the Mermaid.
FEMALE: Jack and the Beanstalk.
MALE: Kiku and Isamu.
FEMALE: The King and the Chorus Girl.
MALE: Night and the City.
FEMALE: Foot and Mouth.
MALE: The Flame and the Flesh.
FEMALE: The Flesh and the Devil.
MALE: Forever and a Day.
FEMALE: The Blue and the Gold.
MALE: A Brother and His Younger Sister.
FEMALE: Yolanda and the Thief.
MALE: Toto and Caroline.
FEMALE: Tiko and the Shark.
MALE: Sex and the Single Girl.
FEMALE: McCabe and Mrs. Miller.
MALE: The Pit and the Pendulum.
FEMALE: Crime and Punishment.
MALE: Trials and Tribulations.
FEMALE: X, Y & Zee.
MALE: Romeo, Juliet and Darkness.
FEMALE: Bob and Carol and Ted and Alice.

BLACKOUT

TANTRUM THREE

> A park bench. Seated on it and
> directly facing the audience, two
> men in impeccable black tailcoats,
> top hats held on their laps, canes
> placed securely against the bench.
> THOMAS and FREDERICK. A long pause.

THOMAS: (Sympathetic) Don't feel bad.

FREDERICK: (Surprised) I'm not.

THOMAS: About your grandmother, I mean.

FREDERICK: Yes.

THOMAS: These things happen, you know.

FREDERICK: I know.

THOMAS: (With elegiac solemnity) She was a good woman.

FREDERICK: Who was?

THOMAS: Your grandmother.

FREDERICK: Oh!

> (Pause)

THOMAS: Did you know her long?

FREDERICK: Since childhood.

THOMAS: Ah yes, of course. What are your plans now?

FREDERICK: The same.

THOMAS: Oh! (A pause. Glancing at the sky) Do you think it will rain?

FREDERICK: (Also glancing at the sky) No!

(Pause)

THOMAS: Are you feeling terribly sad?

FREDERICK: (Patient) Not really.

THOMAS: (Manfully refraining a sob) Funerals always make me sad.

FREDERICK: Oh, don't feel bad.

THOMAS: Thank you, I'm not. (Pause) They served some delicious bonbons, afterwards.

FREDERICK: Yes! Simply delicious, weren't they?

THOMAS: (Produces a fistful) Want one?

FREDERICK: (Suspicious and accusatory) No, thank you.

THOMAS: (Guilty) They're only a few! I didn't think they would mind.

FREDERICK: No, of course not.

THOMAS: Are you very angry?

FREDERICK: Not at all.

THOMAS: Do you mind if I have one?

FREDERICK: Please help yourself.

THOMAS: Thank you.

FREDERICK: My pleasure.

THOMAS: You're sure you won't have one?

FREDERICK: Positive.

(Pause)

THOMAS: Do you like my car?

FREDERICK: Very!

THOMAS: Impressive, isn't it?

FREDERICK: Indubitably!

THOMAS: Majestic?

FREDERICK: Irrevocably!

THOMAS: Stupendous?

FREDERICK: Invariably!

THOMAS: Enchanting?

FREDERICK: Incredibly!

THOMAS: Seductive? Alluring? Tempting?
Passionate? Orgiastic?

FREDERICK: No!

THOMAS: No?

FREDERICK: No!

THOMAS: (Thoroughly nonplussed)   Oh!

(Pause)

THOMAS: Don't feel bad.

FREDERICK: (Curt) I'm not.

THOMAS: About Madeleine Plonget, I mean.

FREDERICK: Who?

THOMAS: Madeleine Plonget! Your mistress!

FREDERICK: That wasn't her name.

THOMAS: Of course it was. You told me so your-self.

FREDERICK: (Puzzled) Are you sure?

THOMAS: Dogmatically!

FREDERICK: I always called her "Frou-Frou."

THOMAS: Well, her real name was Madeleine Plonget.

            (Pause)

FREDERICK: What an absolutely ridiculous name!

THOMAS: Whose?

FREDERICK: Madeleine Plonget!

THOMAS: It's not ridiculous.

FREDERICK: Plonget?

THOMAS: Well! Frou-Frou?

            (A snicker is quickly cut short by
            one of FREDERICK's basilisk glances.
            Pause)

FREDERICK: How did she die?

THOMAS: Who?

FREDERICK: Madeleine Plonget!

THOMAS: Why she threw herself from the sixty-seventh floor of the Empire State Building, of course!

FREDERICK: Amazing! (Slight Pause) Why did she do it?

THOMAS: (Incredulous) Because you married Amelie, naturally!

FREDERICK: (Doubtful) Naturally! (Slight pause) That must have been last week, then.

THOMAS: (Solemn nod) Last Friday!

FREDERICK: (Equally solemn nod) Poor Frou-Frou!

THOMAS: Don't feel sad!

FREDERICK: (Kind) I'm not.

THOMAS: Certain?

FREDERICK: Yes! I'm sorry!

        (Pause)

THOMAS: Snuff?

FREDERICK: Thank you.

        (FREDERICK sniffs a pinch)

THOMAS: Don't mention it.

        (THOMAS sniffs a pinch. A WOMAN and
        a LITTLE BOY appear)

BOY: Mommy, is Joey in heaven now?

WOMAN: No dearest, he is not.

BOY: But why not, mommy?

WOMAN: I've told you many times before dear, animals don't go to heaven.

BOY: Why not mommy?

WOMAN: Because animals don't have souls.

BOY: Do we have souls?

WOMAN: Of course, we have souls.

BOY: But Joey was such a nice dog, wasn't he mommy?

WOMAN: Yes, he was.

BOY: He was so nice and pretty, and he always did what we told him, and he never bit anyone. Do you think mommy, maybe God makes a few exceptions for nice dogs like Joey?

WOMAN: No dearest, only people go to heaven. Animals just die. But God remembers them, of course. He remembers even the littlest bird. But they just don't go to heaven!

> (They disappear. A bird suddenly
> alights on FREDERICK's hat with a
> note in its beak. FREDERICK picks it
> up and reads the cover)

FREDERICK: It's for me.

THOMAS: (Very interested) Oh?

FREDERICK: (To bird) Thank you.

(Bird flies away)

THOMAS: Who is it from?

> (FREDERICK shrugs, reads the note
> for a seemingly interminable period,
> while THOMAS grows increasingly
> agitated)

FREDERICK: It's from my wife!

THOMAS: Ah!

FREDERICK: (Drily) She's dying!

THOMAS: (Shocked) Oh!

FREDERICK: Um! Breast cancer!

THOMAS: Oh!

> (THOMAS speechlessly picks the note
> from FREDERICK and also reads it for
> an interminable period. Then, face
> brimming with sympathy, he turns to
> FREDERICK with a pitiful look)

FREDERICK: I don't feel sad.

> (THOMAS, taken aback, sits offendedly
> in his corner. Pause)

FREDERICK: Do you feel sad?

THOMAS: (Broken) Incurably!

FREDERICK: (Sympathetic) I'm very sorry!

> (THOMAS nods appreciatively and cries.
> FREDERICK sits back very uncomfortably)

THOMAS: (Regaining composure) Forgive me!

FREDERICK: Of course!

THOMAS: Silly of me!

FREDERICK: But understandable!

(Pause. FREDERICK feigns a pitiful
face and utters a gurgling sob.
THOMAS quickly clutches FREDERICK's
shoulder with renewed sympathetic
fervour. FREDERICK suddenly stops)

FREDERICK: It's all right, I didn't succeed!

THOMAS: But you tried!

FREDERICK: (Helpless) To no avail!

(Pause)

THOMAS: You don't particularly care, do you?

FREDERICK: Not really!

THOMAS: Why not?

FREDERICK: It's not good for my health!

THOMAS: (Understanding nod) Oh! (Pause) Look,
there's a man running towards us!

FREDERICK: It's my butler.

(Enter JAMES, the BUTLER; breath-
less but reverential. He has a mys-
terious perennial erection, a striped
extension of his colourful trousers)

BUTLER: I beg your pardon sir, allow me to
apologize for my inexcusably abrupt intrusion.

(FREDERICK waits)

BUTLER: I do apologize, sir.

    (FREDERICK nods in satisfaction)

BUTLER: Oh sir, the light that shone from the
shores of Methuselah to the shores of Marrakesh;
the mellifluous orb of sparkling sensuality; the
serene stratosphere of angelic inspiration; the
verdant sibylline ripe with the forbidden fruit;
the irridescent image of intrinsic aqualine
features; the irascible Vesuvius; the melancholy...

FREDERICK: Kindly get to the point, James!

BUTLER: At once sir! She can but barely flicker
her eye-lids, and then only through a super-
human effort. She can but imperceptibly quiver
her lips, and then only to utter the faintest of
syllables. But God strike me down sir, if I be
telling a lie now, for even though she can
neither speak nor see, methinks I did perceive;
indeed, I can avow for it as far as my sight be
within the limits of its miasmical scope, that
your indelible nomenclature, sir, was glued to
her lips, with imperishable impunity. And her
eyes; oh, her eyes sir! They could but only
assert with their disarming endearment what her
lips laboriously did try. Oh sir, her eyes long
for you! Her lips long for you! Her thumping
heart longs for you! Her Tiresian breasts...

FREDERICK: (Shocked) James!

BUTLER: I beg your pardon, sir! I meant no dis-
respect, sir. Rest assured sir, my thoughts are
filled with undying purity!

FREDERICK: Very well, very well, go on!

BUTLER: In short sir, madame wishes to see you
before... before... before she joins the celestial
choir. (Tearful) My virtuous lady wishes your

forgiveness sir. For indeed, it is for that
solitary design that she so anguishedly struggles
on for her last few borrowed minutes!

(He explodes in a torrent of tears)

FREDERICK: (Not impressed) You may tell madame
I shall be along presently.

BUTLER: Very well sir.

(Exits)

THOMAS: Oh Frederick! Oh woe!

FREDERICK: I wonder why she wants my forgiveness.

THOMAS: Ah women! They always want to be forgiven.

FREDERICK: After all, we've only been married
for a week. What could she possibly have done in
one week?

THOMAS: (Venturing an aimless opinion) She might
have used your toothbrush. In error, of course.

FREDERICK: (Considers it, but remains unsatis-
fied, pondering on a thousand and one possible
sins. He finally rises) Well, I suppose we had
better go and see her now. (Suddenly) You did
say that mauve car was yours?

THOMAS: Yes!

FREDERICK: Oh!

THOMAS: Why?

FREDERICK: Three exquisitely beautiful women are
about to steal it!

(A tremendous roar of an engine
is heard)

THOMAS: (Rushing to left) Hey you there! That's
my car you're driving! Ladies! Please wait! Let's
reason it out for a minute! There must be some
mistake! Ladies! (To FREDERICK) Shall we chase
them?

FREDERICK: There's always the insurance money.

THOMAS: True. We might catch them though.

FREDERICK: I would rather not, really. Let's go
see Amelie, instead.

THOMAS: Let's.

(They trot out to right in step)

FREDERICK: On second thought, why not? I mean,
the exercise will do me good.

THOMAS: (Delighted) Oh how capital! But are you
quite certain you wish to?

FREDERICK: Oh yes, quite!

THOMAS: Oh jolly good then!

(They trot out in step, to left.
Almost immediately they return,
gallantly escorting the three ladies,
DORA, CORA and VERA, dressed in
black turn-of-the-century clothes.
They are extremely mirthful)

DORA: (Exaggerated) Oh sir, surely you jest?

THOMAS: (Vain) I assure you madame, it's all
true.

CORA: (Equally exaggerated) Oh but sir, it's so droll!

THOMAS: Yes, isn't it?

(Laughter)

DORA: Oh, what absolutely charming men you are! We are so very fortunate, aren't we? After all, not everyone would have been as understanding as you have!

THOMAS: Think nothing of it madame. Why indeed, we're the fortunate party to have met you delightful ladies!

FREDERICK: My friend has spoken my very thoughts, dearest ladies.

DORA/CORA/VERA: (Together, blushing) Oh sirs! You're too kind!

FREDERICK/THOMAS: Not at all, you exquisite creatures!

DORA/CORA/VERA: (Wild flickering of eyelids) Oh thank you, generous sirs!

FREDERICK/THOMAS: Our pleasure, most delicious morsels!

DORA: (Serious) Ah, but gentlemen, truly; we must reward you in some way, or we shall remain forever in your debt!

THOMAS: (Protesting) Oh sweet ladies, your debt is our credit!

DORA: (Not quite comprehending) Oh how kind you are, sir!

CORA: I have it Dora!

(Some whispering)

DORA: Oh yes!

CORA: (To FREDERICK) Tell me sir, do you enjoy
the fuck?

> (FREDERICK, very taken aback, can
> only mutter a few indistinguishable
> sounds)

CORA: (To THOMAS) And how about you sir?

> (THOMAS has the same response as
> FREDERICK)

CORA: (Very definitively) Vera dearest, I think
the gentlemen would appreciate a fuck! And you do
it so well, my dear; won't you oblige them first?

VERA: (Very hoarse, thrilled to pieces) Oooh
yes!

DORA: Please gentlemen, make yourselves comfortable!

THOMAS: Em! Well! I say! Em! Oh, after you
gentle ladies!

DORA: How gallant!

> (They all sit on the bench very for-
> mally and watch VERA as she daintily
> strips to her undergarments, to the
> delicate strains of a Vivaldi concerto.
> The necessaries discarded, she gently
> bares her torso, back to the audience,
> striking a triumphant pose in her ex-
> quisitely laced pantaloons. The two
> men gape stupidly for a lingering
> minute, open-mouthed, unable to utter
> a word)

VERA: (Dejected) You are disappointed!

> (Crying, she turns towards the audience to reveal the undeniable fact that she is male. FREDERICK finally gathers up enough courage and timidly advances to VERA, as THOMAS throws suspicious glances at his two companions. FREDERICK clears his throat noisily in protest, but is still unable to speak. VERA, with a sudden fervour, throws herself against FREDERICK and kisses him passionately on the mouth. FREDERICK can only grin sheepishly, hardly able to conceal his embarrassment. He then unreasonably but with an impulsive curiosity, strokes VERA's chest. VERA, encouraged, leads him by the hand to the left, and they exit. Almost immediately offstage...)

FREDERICK: (Loudly protesting) Eh, I think I'd rather not!

> (VERA can be heard crying anguishedly. The two ladies get up sadly, gather VERA's garments and exit dejectedly as Vivaldi's concerto comes to an end. FREDERICK enters, and the two men look at each other for a long time, pondering)

THOMAS: I say, that was perverse.

FREDERICK: Very untoward.

THOMAS: (Suddenly anxious) Is my car still there?

FREDERICK: Hmmm! Yes, I think so. (Slight pause) Well, shall we go and see Amelie now?

THOMAS: Who?

FREDERICK: My wife.

THOMAS: Pray let's.

> (As they are about to exit to the
> right, a great rumbling commotion
> is heard offstage, amidst the cries
> of a seemingly large crowd. A
> frightening organ announces the
> entrance of a huge BISHOP dressed
> majestically in glittering silvery
> robes, with a gigantic mitre, an
> imposing crosier, and the omni-
> present episcopal ring. He is black,
> and his face is painted in pallid
> deathly white stripes. There is a
> sudden hush as he signals the imagin-
> ary crowd to quiet down. The BISHOP,
> eyes ablaze with a fearful fire,
> recites the Pater Noster in a terrify-
> ing sonorous voice, and the crowd is
> heard chanting meekly in response)

BISHOP: Oremnus: Pater noster qui es in coelis.

CROWD: Pater Noster qui es in coelis.

BISHOP: Sanctificetur Nomen tuum: adveniat
regnum tuum.

CROWD: Sanctificetur Nomen tuum: adveniat
regnum tuum.

BISHOP: Fiat voluntas tua, sicut in coelo et in
terra.

CROWD: Fiat voluntas tua, sicut in coelo et in
terra.

BISHOP: Panem nostrum quotidianum da nobis hodie.

CROWD: Panem nostrum quotidianum da nobis hodie.

BISHOP: Et dimitte nobis debita nostra.

CROWD: Et dimitte nobis debita nostra.

BISHOP: Sicut et nos dimittimus debitoribus nostris.

CROWD: Sicut et nos dimittimus debitoribus nostris.

> (As the CROWD is about to chant the word "dimittimus" JC suddenly rushes in complete with crown and thorns and halo, extremely anxious and exhausted. He falls on his knees before the BISHOP, panting breathlessly. Clutching the BISHOP's robe, he cries unabashedly)

JC: My father! My mother! Where are they? You must have seen them! Please, tell me where they are. Please! I must find them!

> (The BISHOP continues praying in silence, completely unmoved. JC gets up and stumbles out crying)

JC: Mama! Papa! Where are you? Please come back! Please! Mama! Papa! Mama! Papa!

> (A moment of hushed silence as the organ slowly rises again, stopping jarringly a couple of times, like a record going at a reduced speed. The BISHOP glares out terribly, then disappears. THOMAS and FREDERICK remain stunned out of their wits. They walk around aimlessly for a while)

FREDERICK: May I have one of those bonbons please?

THOMAS: Certainly!

>   (THOMAS dips into a pocket and
>   brings out a different assortment
>   in error. FREDERICK picks one and
>   examines it silently)

THOMAS: (Guilty) I took a few of those as well.
(Slight pause) Do you think they mind?

FREDERICK: Do they know?

THOMAS: I don't think so.

FREDERICK: In that case, they don't mind. Let's
go and see Amelie now.

THOMAS: (Not understanding immediately, he takes
his time to shine with comprehension) Your wife?

FREDERICK: (Smiling) Yes!

THOMAS: By all means. How is she by the way?
I haven't seen her for a long time.

FREDERICK: (Kindly) I don't think you've ever
met Amelie. She's dying.

THOMAS: (Touched with remorse) Oh, I say, I
am sorry.

FREDERICK: Thank you, but that's all right.
We've only been married a week.

THOMAS: Oh!

>   (JAMES, the BUTLER, rushes in amidst
>   bounteous tears. His erection is now
>   bent)

BUTLER: Oh please forgive me sir! I beg of you
sir, do not look too harshly upon me as a result

of what I am forced to relate to you. I know I shall never forgive myself for this sir. (Another torrent of tears, then finally with great calamity) Oh sir, the light has been snuffed out!

FREDERICK: I beg your pardon?

BUTLER: Madame, sir, is gone.

FREDERICK: Gone? Where?

    (BUTLER glances heavenwards.
    FREDERICK's patience is all gone)

FREDERICK: Well, for heaven's sake, James, kindly get to the point.

BUTLER: (Pitifully abject) Madame is dead sir!

FREDERICK: Ah! (Pause) Very well. Thank you, James. You may go!

BUTLER: (Astonished at the reaction) As you wish, sir!

    (He exits. Pause)

THOMAS: Don't feel bad.

FREDERICK: (Exasperated) I'm not.

THOMAS: (Quickly) About your wife, I mean.

FREDERICK: (Patiently, but without anger) I tell you I'm not. I never gave a damn about her, or any of the others for that matter. And I still don't. Their deaths mean nothing to me. I really am sorry Thomas, but it doesn't make much of a difference one way or the other.

THOMAS: Why did you marry Amelie?

FREDERICK: She wanted to.

THOMAS: And you?

FREDERICK: I didn't mind.

THOMAS: But why bother?

FREDERICK: It made her happy.

THOMAS: Oh!

(Pause)

FREDERICK: It's all the same to me. Everything
is the same.

THOMAS: Not everything.

FREDERICK: For instance?

THOMAS: Vera!

FREDERICK: Oh, that was only the first shock of
novelty.

(Pause)

THOMAS: Another bonbon?

FREDERICK: Please! The first assortment if you
don't mind.

THOMAS: Of course.

FREDERICK: Thank you.

THOMAS: Not at all. Do you mind if I have one
too?

FREDERICK: Oh really Thomas! Please help
yourself.

THOMAS: Thank you. (Pause) It's cold.

FREDERICK: Yes.

THOMAS: Do you suppose it will last?

FREDERICK: (Melancholy) Yes.

           (Pause)

THOMAS: What do you make of events?

FREDERICK: They happen. (Long pause) You know
Thomas, I'm happy. I am, I truly am happy.
(He gets up, walks to the obstacle in the background, inspects it at length and pondering he
speaks with deliberate intensity) I am inexpli-
cably, violently, insanely, thrillingly,
deliriously happy! (He sits) Yes. I-am-happy!

           (Suddenly the stage is plunged in
           darkness as a loud feverish radio
           broadcast is heard)

ANNOUNCER: We interrupt this programme to bring
you the latest on the lunar expedition. It's been
found! It's been found, at last! The universal
truth has finally been revealed to our astronauts.
It is now an accomplished fact that Jesus Christ
was the actual leader of the Christians. We repeat,
it has been discovered beyond any doubt that Jesus
Christ actually did lead the Christians in revolt.
We shall have further details in our 6:30 news. We
now resume our regular programme.

           (The lights slowly dim back to reveal
           an empty stage, with the exception of
           a little red ball, centre stage.

               BLACKOUT

A siren. Long and loud)

73

TANTRUM FOUR

Incessant grinding roaring noises, which grow more fervent and loud near the end. A voice, on tape, begins a countdown, starting at 244.

COUNTDOWN 244

A MAN, naked, is lying asleep on the floor. Close to him, a neatly arranged pile of clothes.

COUNTDOWN 228

The MAN is still asleep.

COUNTDOWN 206

The MAN wakes up, but remains immobile.

COUNTDOWN 185

The MAN slowly, reluctantly, raises his head and looks around him. He sees the clothes. He stares at them intently.

COUNTDOWN 163

The MAN feels weary. He dozes off again.

COUNTDOWN 146

The MAN sleepily raises himself half-way. He stares at the clothes, his eyes falling shut. He listens to the countdown.

COUNTDOWN 127

The MAN dozes off again.

COUNTDOWN 102

The MAN reluctantly gets up again. He finally
decides to move. He moves a leg. Thinks. He
moves the other. Stares sleepily at the clothes.
Finally crawls to the pile and listlessly looks
through it. He finds a pair of underpants. He
manages to put them on. Instantly he falls asleep.

COUNTDOWN 71

He lazily wakes up and dazedly looks for a vest.
He finds one. He wearily puts it on. He finds
he has the wrong side on. He slowly takes it off.
He puts it on again, correct side.

COUNTDOWN 59

He picks up a shirt, puts it on and buttons it
wrong. He notices. He is frustrated but too
tired to bother. He finally decides to unbutton
it.

COUNTDOWN 48

He starts buttoning the shirt again. He can't.
The buttons don't seem to get into place. He
suddenly realizes this as if for the first time
and finally seems to be aware of the countdown
and the seriousness of his situation. He is now
jolted out of his daze.

COUNTDOWN 41

He tries the buttons again. He starts to get
increasingly frustrated. He can't get them into
place. He keeps trying. He keeps fumbling with
the buttons. He starts to panic.

COUNTDOWN 35

He finally manages to get a couple of buttons in place. He discovers that the shirt doesn't fit him at all. It's too small. The collar button is impossible. The sleeve buttons haven't a chance. He is now desperate.

COUNTDOWN 27

He leaves the shirt. Frantically, he starts to fumble with the socks. He somehow gets them on.

COUNTDOWN 24

He hurriedly puts on the trousers. Takes an eternity with the zipper. It is stuck. He is going insane. The zipper obstinate as ever. He makes a super-human effort. He pulls with all his strength. He pulls and pulls. Finally, finally he gets it closed. The trousers are far too large for him. He can't be bothered.

COUNTDOWN 20

The countdown from 20 on is now being screamed terribly and lengthier pauses are taken between numbers. The MAN tries the tie. He can't remember how to tie it.

COUNTDOWN 13

He frenziedly attempts various knots. None of them work. Not one works.

COUNTDOWN 18

He stops. Hands trembling. His whole body is shaking. Frightfully aware of the countdown.

COUNTDOWN 17

He tries once more. Very, very patiently.

COUNTDOWN 16

He keeps trying. Very slowly.

COUNTDOWN 15

He pretends he has plenty of time. He keeps at
it studiously.

COUNTDOWN 14

He still takes his time. On purpose. If only
to get it right.

COUNTDOWN 13

He still can't get it right.

COUNTDOWN 12

Becoming extremely angry, he frustratedly jerks
at it. He decides to leave it for the time being.

COUNTDOWN 11

He goes for the jacket. Somehow his arms can't
seem to get into the sleeves.

COUNTDOWN 10

His arms persist in missing the sleeves. He
furiously throws it aside.

COUNTDOWN 9

He tries the shoes. The laces are tied. He can't
seem to get them loose.

COUNTDOWN 8

He starts biting at the laces. Impossible knots.

COUNTDOWN 7

He miraculously gets the laces on one shoe untied.
He greedily tries on the shoe. It's painfully
tight. His foot won't go in.

COUNTDOWN 6

He tortures his foot into it. He refuses to give
up. He finally gets it on. Extreme pain.

COUNTDOWN 5

He tries to tie the laces. Aware of the countdown.
Furious. Crazed. He fumbles. He works at tremendous speed.

COUNTDOWN 4

Impossible. Laces won't tie. How to knot? He
attempts a simple knot. Shaky fingers. Maddening
speed.

COUNTDOWN 3

Still at the laces. He makes a split second
decision to try the other shoe. Even worse.

COUNTDOWN 2

One more time at laces. Aware of countdown.
Tremendous effort. All fingers. Shaking.
Trembling. Frightened.

COUNTDOWN 1

The MAN immediately stops dressing. His eyes are
wide open with horror. He sits motionless and
terrified. The grinding roaring noises abruptly
stop. Absolute silence.

The MAN painfully, torturously, widens his mouth
and hurls out one prolonged, desperate, noiseless
scream. In total silence.

> (A siren. Simultaneous with the
> scream. Very long. Very loud.
>
> BLACKOUT
>
> Silence.
>
> LIGHTS
>
> The stage is empty with the excep-
> tion of the LITTLE GIRL. She stands
> facing the audience, with a large
> red ball. Very slowly she presents
> the ball to the audience. She smiles
> faintly, enigmatically)
>
> BLACKOUT

THE END

BRANDY

THE PLACE:

A jungle. A clearing in the middle. A large rock
dead centre. A historic branch somewhere to the
left.

THE TIME:

Late afternoon.

THE TEMPERATURE:

90 degrees Fahrenheit.

MORE ON THE CHARACTERS

JEREMIAH.....The Big Guy. A native tribal chief.
          Looks mean and scary. Lots of muscles.
          Clothing: a pair of khaki shorts.

HUBERT.....The Little Man. A spectacled, skinny
          nobody. Looks like a chicken.
          Clothing: baggy pants, a ruffled short-
          sleeved shirt with a couple of missing
          buttons, and running-shoes.

THE BLONDE.....The Dizzy Dame. Beautiful, sexy,
          small breasts. Not much else.
          Clothing: safari coat, shorts and hat.
          Underneath, colorful underwear which
          never come off.

THE BRUNETTE.....The Dumb Broad. Beautiful, sexy,
          big breasts. Not much else.
          Clothing: seductive sleeveless blouse
          (no bra underneath), tight fitting
          jeans rolled up at the legs, and nifty
          shoes.

SCENE ONE

All stage lights and house lights are
on before the audience is admitted.
No curtains may be used.

Without warning, JEREMIAH jumps onstage
from up right and makes a mad dash
towards the audience.

HUBERT takes one giant step out from
upstage right, standing rigid with a
cool, steely look, gun in hand, arm
extended right out, and fires six quick
shots in JEREMIAH's back.

JEREMIAH falls downstage centre, dead
with the first bullet, his limp body
going through uncontrollable contortions as the other five bullets hit
him.

Furious dramatic music a la James Bond
blares out as HUBERT puts the gun back
in his pocket and walks towards the
dead JEREMIAH, looking down at him with
cool disdain.

Without warning, HUBERT jumps down on
JEREMIAH in a sudden animal rage, and
begins to strangle him, jump on him,
kick him, beat him up; emitting violent
growls and cursing out in a wild unintelligible gibberish.

All the lights pound on and off during
this sequence for about thirty seconds
before blacking out.

HUBERT continues for another five
seconds in the dark, then stops.

The music continues, louder than ever.

BLACKOUT

SCENE TWO

Jungle noises, the most prominent of
which is the incessant howling of a
nearby wolf.

JEREMIAH is sitting on the rock,
directly facing the audience.

JEREMIAH glares threateningly at the
audience emitting fearful growls every
once in a while. He carries this on for
some twenty seconds, then starts to
cool off, but very, very slowly. He
looks out rather seriously for a split
second before his look eases into a
smile...a knowing smile that develops
into a huge, broad grin.

He quickly cuts the grin with a warning
glare and emits another admonishing
growl.

He has an unforgiving temper, but the
glare goes through another slow tran-
sition which expands to an even huger,
broader grin.

Once again, without warning, his temper
takes over and two quick growls are
snapped out. His face glaring out with

85

one last look of caution directed
at the audience. But JEREMIAH is
now fully confident and satisfied,
his face once again enveloped by
that huge broad grin.

He rolls his head sideways, oozing
charm and cuddly cuteness, as he
proudly announces to the audience
in a big, self-confident manner...

JEREMIAH: I got a Volkswagen Van. (Slight pause)

HUBERT: (Offstage. In a long, melodic, almost
unbelieving tone) Yeaahhh?

JEREMIAH: (Equally melodic and self-confident)
Yeaahhh! (Slight pause. Happier and prouder than
ever) I like my Volkswagen Van. (Slight pause)

HUBERT: (Offstage) Yeaahhh?

JEREMIAH: Yeaahhh! (Slight pause) That Volkswagen Van was the first car I ever drove. (Slight
pause)

HUBERT: (Offstage) Yeaahhh?

JEREMIAH: Yeaahhh! (Slight pause) The first
time I ever drove that Volkswagen Van was across
a desert. (Slight pause)

HUBERT: (Offstage) Yeaahhh?

JEREMIAH: Yeaahhh! (Slight pause) It was my
pappy's book-keeper who taught me how to drive
that Volkswagen Van. (Slight pause)

HUBERT: (Offstage) Yeaahhh?

JEREMIAH: Yeaahhh! (Slight pause) He taught me
how to drive on my pappy's Volkswagen Van. (Slight

pause)

HUBERT: (Making his way in from the thick of the jungle, looking edgy and nervous and liberally chomping on his fingernails; more incredulous than ever)   Naaaaa!

JEREMIAH: (Emphatically, self-confident, melodic and cheerful)   Yeaahhh! (Slight pause) That Volkswagen Van used to belong to my pappy, but he gave it to me, so now it's my Volkswagen Van. (Slight pause)

HUBERT: Naaaaa!

JEREMIAH: Yeaahhh! (Slight pause) My pappy has two Volkswagen Vans, that's how come I got one. (Slight pause)

HUBERT: Naaaaa!

JEREMIAH: Yeaahhh! (Slight pause) Now we both got Volkswagen Vans. (Slight pause)

HUBERT: Yeaahhhh?

JEREMIAH: Yeaahhh! (Slight pause. JEREMIAH, by this time is just brimming with proud cheeriness and has acquired a glint of mischief in his eyes) My pappy's Volkswagen Van is a huge son-of-a-bitch, but mine's got a radio! (Slight pause)

HUBERT: (By this time, having developed a whole new set of nervous tics, can't swallow JEREMIAH much longer and decides to challenge him)   Oh yeaahhh?

JEREMIAH: (Still smiling)   You betcha yeaahhh!

HUBERT: (Bigger)   Oh yeaaahhhh?

JEREMIAH: (Huger than ever)   Yeaaaahhhhh!

> (HUBERT gets the message
> and goes back to his
> corner with another set
> of nervous tics. A pause
> as JEREMIAH sits back
> once again happily con-
> fident, and HUBERT, the
> wreck, chomps away on a
> few more fingernails)

HUBERT: (Having just acquired a brilliant idea,
decides to play JEREMIAH's game, boasting
proudly)   I got a bottle of 7-UP.

JEREMIAH: (Incredulous jeer)   Well no shit?

HUBERT: No!

JEREMIAH: (Jeering away) Well, whadda ya know?

HUBERT: Whadda ya mean?

JEREMIAH: 7-UP, huh?

HUBERT: Yeah, a whole bottle.   With the 7-UP
still in it.

JEREMIAH: Ah, come on.

HUBERT: Whadda ya mean, "come on?"

JEREMIAH: I don't believe you.

HUBERT: Oh, you don't, huh?

JEREMIAH: No, I don't.

HUBERT: Oh yeah?

JEREMIAH: Yeah!

HUBERT: Yeah?

JEREMIAH: Yeah!

HUBERT: Well, I'll show you then.

JEREMIAH: Yeah, you do that. You show me.

HUBERT: Okay, I will. (Takes a few steps but stops) Wait a minute, you show me your Volkswagen Van first. Before I show you any of my stuff, I wanna see that Van of yours.

JEREMIAH: (Not liking it) What's the matter, don't you believe me?

HUBERT: No, I didn't say that.

JEREMIAH: (Threatening) Well, that's what you meant, didn't you?

HUBERT: No I didn't, no I didn't, I just wanna see it, that's all.

JEREMIAH: (Big) What for?

HUBERT: (Little, almost whispering; becomes very congenial) Well, what do you wanna see my bottle for? I mean, there's only one reason why you wanna see it for and that's 'cause you don't believe me, 'cause if I gotta show you my bottle first for you to believe me, then that means that you don't believe me. Right?

JEREMIAH: Yeah, that's right.

HUBERT: You don't believe me then!!

JEREMIAH: No I don't.

HUBERT: Oh, I see.

JEREMIAH: (Big jeering smile) Yeah!

HUBERT: (Enraged) Listen Jeremiah, I don't like
the way you're shoving me around all the time,
okay?

JEREMIAH: You don't huh?

HUBERT: No I don't.

JEREMIAH: Ohhh? Well, what are you gonna do 'bout
it, Hubert? Huh? (Grabbing HUBERT by the scruff
of the shirt, JEREMIAH is now very, very angry)
Come on Hubert, you tell me, just what you gonna
do 'bout it!

BLACKOUT

(Some African music)

SCENE THREE

        JEREMIAH is lying dead in
        the same position where he
        fell in SCENE ONE. HUBERT
        is holding his gun and
        looking down at him, very
        dazed. The BLONDE, who had
        fallen down on her posterior,
        is now sitting up and also
        looking very dazed.

BLONDE: (Whimpers, pointing an accusatory finger at JEREMIAH) Eh, eh, eh, eh, eh, you killed him.

> (Starts bawling out like a little
> girl; it was a great loss)

HUBERT: Huh? Oh yeah!

BLONDE: (Suddenly capricious, she stops crying and begins to talk extremely rapidly from this point onwards, firing questions at a machine-gun pace, creating verbal havoc not only on herself but also on the bewildered HUBERT) Oh Christ! Now what am I gonna do?

HUBERT: Let me help you up.

BLONDE: No, leave me alone.

HUBERT: All right.

BLONDE: What are you doing?

HUBERT: Gym.

BLONDE: What?

HUBERT: I teach.

BLONDE: Where's your class?

HUBERT: Oh, I left them somewhere back there. They can do all that stuff by themselves. Who are you?

BLONDE: (Who has been pacing, moving, jittering at a whirlwind pace all over the stage, is now crouching next to JEREMIAH) I loved him. Oh God, I loved him.

HUBERT: It's a nice jungle.

BLONDE: Thanks for saving my life.

HUBERT: Oh sure.

BLONDE: (Hysterical but nowhere near where she's going to be two minutes later) You have to re-ciprocate, don't you?

HUBERT: (Getting seduced into the hysteria, finds himself talking equally rapidly, in spite of his dazed condition) What?

BLONDE: When you're in love, I mean it's not just a one way deal, you know? You have to be loved back, even if sometimes, you know?

HUBERT: Yeah!

BLONDE: I was crazy in love with him, but d'you think he cared? He had a girl in New York.

HUBERT: Oh yeah, I hear New York's pretty tough these days.

BLONDE: That's not the point. He didn't give a shit if I was alive and in pain. I hurt with love for him and he never once sent me any flowers.

> (Gives the dead JEREMIAH a slap
> on the head. He momentarily opens
> his eyes)

HUBERT: You know that branch is at least a hundred years old?

BLONDE: What? Listen, there was a fire.

HUBERT: (Alarmed) Where?

BLONDE: Back there, it just rose up all over and covered everything. I had to run.

HUBERT: Is it out now?

BLONDE: No, it's still on.

(The valiant HUBERT makes
a mad dash out)

BLONDE: Oh God, I loved him. (Removes blouse)
That bastard didn't even care though. He just
didn't, didn't, didn't.

HUBERT: (Back again, he couldn't find the fire)
What are you doing?

BLONDE: Don't you want to make love?

HUBERT: Oh...yeah sure. (Unbuttons shirt)

BLONDE: And he kept talking about this girl all the
time, I mean he could have at least spared me that.
I can't have orgasms.

HUBERT: Oh well.

BLONDE: I mean, I got feelings too. (About to kiss
him) Look, I'm sorry but I don't feel like it any
more.

HUBERT: Oh! (Rebuttons his shirt)

BLONDE: But I'll repay you some other time. For
saving my life. I promise. Oh, I could have died
for him; he knew it too but he just didn't even
give a shit.

HUBERT: Well, that's life for you.

BLONDE: (Really jumpy now) Gimme a branch, gimme
a branch, one that's historic.

HUBERT: Here take this one. Tarzan was on this once.

BLONDE: But is it historic? Hey, do you think my
breasts are small? (Commences to unbutton his shirt)

HUBERT: Well, they're pretty small but there's nothing wrong with that.

BLONDE: (Begins to fondle his chest) Why do you teach?

HUBERT: It's a job.

BLONDE: (Begins to pinch his nipples) Do you like it?

HUBERT: Oh,I've seen it all before. It gets boring after a while so I dump the whole pack way out there, back there somewhere, and let 'em sweat it out for a coupla days.

>   (She starts licking his nipples
>   wetly. Needless to say, HUBERT
>   is flustered)

HUBERT: Then I go and pick 'em up again. I got a Volkswagen Van, did you see it?

BLONDE: (Mouth full, now violently nibbling on the nipples) No.

HUBERT: (Finding it a little too strange for comfort, he tries desperately to divert her attention) Oh, it's just out there by a cliff. I like my Volkswagen Van, that was the first car I ever drove, right across a desert, my father's book-keeper taught me how to drive, whoo whoo.

>   (Jumps nervously beyond her
>   immediate grasp)

BLONDE: (Pointing at JEREMIAH) That bastard used to drive trucks. Nitro-glycerine. We were on the road for three days. Drove like a madman, never stopped either, only to have a pee once in a while, and only when he wanted to, he never stopped for me. Christ, it's hell holding it.

(Starts chasing him again)

BLONDE: The nitro blew up one day, so we had to
walk the rest of the way, I mean it wasn't my
fault, was it? Oh, it's terrible walking in
jungles, you hear these drums all the time and
you expect a bunch of cannibals to come down on
you everywhere you go. Ugh, humans, they must be
salty!

> (This last, a seductive
> statement, now having caught
> up with him)

HUBERT: (Defensive) They're okay with 7-UP.

BLONDE: (Rapidly removing her shorts, revealing
multi-colored underwear) Listen, I feel like it
again, do you mind?

HUBERT: Huh? Yeah, let's go. (Off with his shirt)

BLONDE: Let's do it on this rock, okay? Oh God, I
love rocks. It's hard but it takes care of the
guilt.

HUBERT: The rock?

BLONDE: Yeah, it's sort of punishment and pleasure
all in one, you know, lookit let's kiss, no wait,
I don't feel like it, are you angry?

HUBERT: No, are you?

BLONDE: Just upset, I always get upset when I can't
make up my mind, do you think it's because I'm a
woman?

HUBERT: Getting upset?

BLONDE: (Really putting on some mileage in her
verbal assault) No, no, no, not making up my mind.

HUBERT: (No choice but to join the oral race now) Oh no, I doubt it. Listen...

BLONDE: I'm scared, I'm scared, I'm scared, come here, I wanna cry, come here please, no, no, no, over your head, over your head, I wanna cry over your head, I like heads when they're against my chest, are my breasts very small?

HUBERT: Yes but...

BLONDE: (Frenziedly) Oh God, but they're soft, they're so soft.

HUBERT: (Equally frenzied) Yeah, that's what I was gonna say.

BLONDE: I mean, if I was to put in all that syn-thetic stuff like silicon and what, I mean they'll be hard like rocks, oh God, rocks, I just love sitting on rocks, don't you? It's those edges, they hurt but I deserve it. (Suddenly screaming) Where is it, where is it?

HUBERT: What, what?

BLONDE: Your car, your car, oh, your car.

HUBERT: Over there, right there, it's a van, a Volkswagen...

BLONDE: Oh I wanna see it, I wanna see it, I wanna see it. Oh God, do you like me when I spread my legs like this? It's very sexy I know, but these breasts ruin everything. Still, I've got unisex appeal, don't you think? Oh suck me, suck me, suck me.

HUBERT: Aie, aie, my hair.

BLONDE: Oh your hair, your hair. Oh I'm sorry, did I hurt you? Oh I'm so sorry, I won't pull again,

I promise. Oh God, suck me, please, please,go on,
suck me, give me head, oh please please suck suck
suck me. No, I mean it, I'm serious, really, go
ahead, go on, it's all yours, go ahead and suck
me, I'll let you, really, honest, yeah yeah, no I
won't pull your hair, oh please suck me, I'll
really like that, yeah, go on, yeah honest, suck
me.

> (HUBERT is convinced of her
> willingness and so he plunges
> in)

BLONDE: Oh, no, no, no, what are you doing? I gotta
see your car first, I wanna see it, where is it,
where is it, over there, come and show me, no I'll
find it, you stay here and get ready for me, I'll
go alone, oh God I love cars, don't go away, I'll
be back, but I wanna know the truth first, you
really don't mind my breasts do you, I mean will
they do, seeing we're in the jungle and all that,
I mean if nothing better comes along, will you
take them, oh say yes, say yes, say yes, please?!

HUBERT: Yes!

BLONDE: Oh goody, I'm so happy, I'll marry you, in
two weeks, I promise, no, two months, I should have
everything straightened out by then. Oh, but God
I forgot, I love that bastard.

HUBERT: The New York guy?

BLONDE: He's not from New York, he's just got a
girl there. Oh I still love him.

HUBERT: Yeah, but he's dead.

BLONDE: Murder! Killing! Death! (Violently
kisses him on the chest) Oh God! I'll be back,
wait for me, don't go away.

                    (Rushes out, then immediately
                    rushes back in)

BLONDE: Oh, but I forgot, how will you, how will
I, how will you, how will I recognize you?

HUBERT: Don't worry, I'll recognize your breasts.

BLONDE: Oh yes of course that's true.

                    (Another mad rush out, followed
                    by an instant mad rush in)

BLONDE: I'm also blonde, don't forget that, okay,
okay, okay?

HUBERT: Yeah, yeah, okay, okay.

BLONDE: Oh God, I'll be back.

                    (Zooms out. A pause. HUBERT is
                    very dazed. JEREMIAH, who had
                    made two previous attempts to
                    get up during the BLONDE's two
                    false exits, and quickly played
                    dead in her entrances, cautiously
                    rises now and is standing to one
                    side with a sly smile)

HUBERT: (Seeing JEREMIAH) Oh, don't tell me I
missed!

JEREMIAH: Yeah, you missed all right. Do you
want my autograph?

HUBERT: Yeah, listen...

JEREMIAH: Got a pen?

HUBERT: No, listen, give me some advice, will you?

JEREMIAH: (Who has produced his own pen and paper now) Shall I write it down?

HUBERT: No, just say it. Listen...Oh, I got a headache.

JEREMIAH: Don't hang around with dizzy blondes.

HUBERT: Oh her. Yeah, did you see her breasts? They're really small, aren't they? I mean you really gotta look for them.

JEREMIAH: Yeah, well the jungle does strange things to people. Oh, by the way, she also steals car keys.

HUBERT: Jeez,now you tell me! Christ! (Rushes out)

JEREMIAH: Hey, what about my autograph?

BLACKOUT

(African music)

SCENE FOUR

JEREMIAH is sitting serenely on the rock, with his sly smile. HUBERT is nervously pacing up and down, deep in thought.

JEREMIAH suddenly slaps his head, instantly killing a fly. He picks it up, inspects it, then throws it right next to HUBERT, maintaining all along, that sly smile of his.

                    HUBERT contemplates JEREMIAH's
                    uncouthness.

                    JEREMIAH keeps on smiling mis-
                    chievously, waiting for an
                    appropriate moment.

JEREMIAH: I hate Tarzan.

HUBERT: (Weary) Ah, come on.

JEREMIAH: I do. I hate the son-of-a-bitch.

HUBERT: Ah, get away.

JEREMIAH: Listen, Hubert, I don't like the guy.

HUBERT: Go on.

JEREMIAH: Hubert, I said I don't like that mother.

HUBERT: Ah, don't be ridiculous.

JEREMIAH: What's so ridiculous about that?

HUBERT: Well, that you don't like him.

JEREMIAH: That ain't ridiculous.

HUBERT: Oh it is, it is.

JEREMIAH: Oh yeah?

HUBERT: Yeah.

JEREMIAH: Ridiculous, huh?

HUBERT: Yeah.

JEREMIAH: You think so?

HUBERT: Yeah, I do.

JEREMIAH: No fooling?

HUBERT: No.

JEREMIAH: (Getting mad) You sure now?

HUBERT: Yeah, sure I'm sure.

JEREMIAH: Think again.

HUBERT: All right, I will.

JEREMIAH: (Mad) Well?

HUBERT: Well?

JEREMIAH: (Really mad) Well, what did you think!

HUBERT: (Thinks better than to answer him) Aw, nothing.

> (Though he can't resist
> uttering a silent "ridiculous"
> as soon as JEREMIAH turns his
> back)

JEREMIAH: See, I told you, you don't know what you're talking about.

HUBERT: Oh I don't, huh?

JEREMIAH: No you don't.

HUBERT: Well, why don't I?

JEREMIAH: 'Cause you think Tarzan is some hot shit, that's why.

HUBERT: Well, he is.

JEREMIAH: See what I mean?

HUBERT: So what's wrong with him?

JEREMIAH: Everything.

HUBERT: All right, name me one.

JEREMIAH: All right, I will.

HUBERT: I dare you.

JEREMIAH: Okay, I will.

HUBERT: Okay, I dare you.

JEREMIAH: Okay, he don't look like no ape-man to me.

HUBERT: Sure he does.

JEREMIAH: No he don't.

HUBERT: He does so.

JEREMIAH: (Violent) He fucking don't.

HUBERT: Well, why don't he?

JEREMIAH: Because!

HUBERT: Oh yeah?

JEREMIAH: Yeah!

HUBERT: Yeah?

JEREMIAH: Yeah!

HUBERT: That's no reason.

JEREMIAH: Sure it is.

HUBERT: No it ain't.

JEREMIAH: Well, why ain't it, Hubert?

HUBERT: 'Cause you gotta have facts, that's why it ain't, Jeremiah.

JEREMIAH: Well, I got facts.

HUBERT: Oh yeah?

JEREMIAH: Yeah!

HUBERT: Yeah?

JEREMIAH: Yeah!

HUBERT: Well, I don't believe you, Jeremiah.

JEREMIAH: You better believe me, Hubert.

HUBERT: I fucking don't, Jeremiah.

JEREMIAH: Why the fuck don't you, Hubert?

HUBERT: 'Cause you're full of shit, Jeremiah.

JEREMIAH: Oh I am, huh?

HUBERT: That's right, you are.

JEREMIAH: Well, you don't say?

HUBERT: Yeah, I just did, Jeremiah.

JEREMIAH: Well, how about that?

HUBERT: Yeah, how 'bout it!

JEREMIAH: I'm full of shit, huh?

HUBERT: Yeaahhh!

JEREMIAH: Well, holy shit!

HUBERT: No, just a piece of shit.

JEREMIAH: That's not what you said before.

HUBERT: Sure I did.

JEREMIAH: No, you didn't.

HUBERT: I did.

JEREMIAH: You didn't.

HUBERT: So what did I say?

JEREMIAH: You said I was full of shit.

HUBERT: That's exactly what I said.

JEREMIAH: You didn't the second time.

HUBERT: I did so.

JEREMIAH: No, you didn't.

HUBERT: I did.

JEREMIAH: You said I was a piece of shit.

HUBERT: So what's the difference?

JEREMIAH: (Furious rage) It's not the same thing.

HUBERT: What's not the same thing?

JEREMIAH: Full of shit and a piece of shit.

HUBERT: I don't see any difference.

JEREMIAH: Sure you don't.

HUBERT: No, I don't.

JEREMIAH: That's what I said, you don't.

HUBERT: Okay, so I don't.

JEREMIAH: Yeah, because you're stupid, that's why you don't.

HUBERT: You calling me stupid?

JEREMIAH: Yeaahhh, I'm calling you stupid, stupid!

HUBERT: (Exploding with pent-up rage) You know something, my mother used to call me that all the time. Come here stupid, go there stupid, stupid this, stupid that, yeah stupid, no stupid, stupid, stupid, stupid, stupid, stupid, stupid! Aaaaaaaa!

(African music)

BLACKOUT

SCENE FIVE

    JEREMIAH is luxuriating in the
    intricate mechanics of lighting
    a cigar. Suddenly the BRUNETTE
    rushes in out of nowhere, with
    a blood-curdling yell, and goes
    straight for JEREMIAH with her
    raised machete. JEREMIAH ducks
    just in time.

JEREMIAH: Hey, watch that knife! Watch it! Listen, I got a lot of money.

BRUNETTE: (Stops momentarily) What do you want?

JEREMIAH: You.

BRUNETTE: (Another headlong lunge) No!

JEREMIAH: Wait a minute, wait a minute, I can give you nice dresses, rubies, diamonds, mink coats, gourmet dinners, palaces, villas, yachts, private planes... (At this point tne pursued gradually becomes the pursuer) ...parties every night...(Aside)...my uncle just died last week... (Back to the BRUNETTE)...I can introduce you to famous movie stars, take you to beautiful cities, gold, all the money you want, Rolls Royce, chic clothing, round beds, Pierre Cardin Bed-sheets, delicious foods, fur lining on your toilet seat, parties with kings and princes, everything, any-thing, sleep with me.

BRUNETTE: (Assuming her Shirley Temple pose) No!

JEREMIAH: Why not?

BRUNETTE: (Fussy) You're ugly!

JEREMIAH: True! But I don't make love more than twice a month, I can promise you that. And re-member, I'll give you everything you want. Now, that's not a bad deal now, is it?

BRUNETTE: (Capricious) Why me?

JEREMIAH: You're pretty.

BRUNETTE: (Shirley Temple at full blast from this point onwards) Yes, but I don't have anything to give you in return.

JEREMIAH: Ohhh, just your body twice a month will be plenty.

BRUNETTE: No! No, that's not fair, I'll be stealing from you.

106

JEREMIAH: (W.C. Fields slowly creeping in) Oh no, no, I can assure you, with my looks, twice a month is too much to ask from anybody. So you see, it'll be me who'll really be doing the stealing.

BRUNETTE: Oooh, you animal. You big, big animal.

JEREMIAH: Yeesss, my mother used to call me that all the time. Animal! Come here animal, go there animal. Listen, I'll throw in a coupla nice boys and girls, what da ya say?

BRUNETTE: No!

JEREMIAH: How about a harem of gigolos?

BRUNETTE: No!

JEREMIAH: Dogs, cats, horses, anything you want?

BRUNETTE: No, I still say it isn't fair.

JEREMIAH: Ohh, you still say it isn't fair. Oh come on, say yes, what the hell. I'll even throw in a coupla puppies, kittens, a box of pigeons, rabbits...

BRUNETTE: Kitties?

JEREMIAH: Yeeesss!

BRUNETTE: Oh okay!

JEREMIAH: Thank you, you're very kind, here have a seat, make yourself comfortable. Listen, I have to deliver this autograph, but I'll be back in a minute. (Stern)

BLONDE: (Offstage. Screaming) I hate you, I hate you, hate, hate, hate, hate, hate, hate.

JEREMIAH: (Quickly assuming his dead man's position) Oh Christ!

> (The BLONDE zooms across the
> stage and exits on the other
> side, then pops her head
> back in to check on the
> BRUNETTE, whom she thought
> she had glimpsed on her way
> out. The BLONDE walks in
> and stares lengthily at the
> BRUNETTE, who giggles back)

BRUNETTE: Hi! (Slight pause as she giggles nervously) He died.

BLONDE: Who?

BRUNETTE: My husband. (Meaning JEREMIAH) We were just married too.

BLONDE: Oh, I'm sorry.

BRUNETTE: Well, not really, he left me a lot of money, you know. So much I don't know what to do with it all. He was sort of nice actually.

BLONDE: Oh?

BRUNETTE: But he was very ugly, the poor dear. I feel sorry for him in a way, and I know, I just know, that I won't be able to enjoy all that money he left me. I'll feel guilty if I do.

> (She immediately sheds her Shirley
> Temple image and rushes headlong
> into her prim socialite)

BRUNETTE: Well, you see, that's why I started doing all this charity work. It keeps me busy and occupied, I feel useful and forget the past. And I'll have you know my charity work isn't anything

of the sort those rich women do. You know, the
handing out the money, and the going to the
meetings, and committees and all that. Oh no. I
haven't given anybody any money. It's all in a
bank in Switzerland. I've just given myself to
my work, body and spirit, but anonymous. I'm a
missionary, you see, and I do all my work manually.
Yes, with my own two hands. Yes, well, it keeps
me strong, healthy and on the go. Oh, I can prove
it too because I sweat a lot. Ugh! As a matter
of fact, I smell a bit now.

> (Beginning to get uncomfortable
> now, quickly switches back to
> her Shirley Temple)

BRUNETTE: Hey, you wanna smell me?

BLONDE: Eh, no.

BRUNETTE: Aw go on, smell me. Here, go ahead,
smell my underarm. Go on.

> (The BLONDE takes two short
> sniffs)

BRUNETTE: Can you smell me? I haven't taken a
bath since yesterday, I haven't had time. I smell,
don't I?

BLONDE: A little.

BRUNETTE: Yeah, well, see, I don't have time to
wash myself, 'cause I'm always so busy. Is it
very bad?

BLONDE: Oh no, it's rather pleasant. One day is
nothing to worry about.

BRUNETTE: Yeah, but in the jungle?

BLONDE: Oh no, it's okay. Really.

BRUNETTE: I don't repulse you, do I?

BLONDE: No, of course not. Don't be silly. Actually a day's sweat is very stimulating sexually.

BRUNETTE: Do you love me?

BLONDE: Yes I do.

> (A passionate kiss. As soon as the kiss is over, they realize what they've just done. All they can do at this point is giggle a lot. They cuddle up together on the rock)

BRUNETTE: (Very chummy) I love you too. Very much. Am I your ideal woman?

BLONDE: Oh yes, you're very ideal. I just adore brunettes.

BRUNETTE: And the sweat?

BLONDE: As long as it's a day old, I'll love that too.

BRUNETTE: My breasts?

BLONDE: Ohhh, just the right size.

BRUNETTE: Would you rather I had bush under my arms?

BLONDE: Oooohh yes, yes, yes, that would really heighten the animal eroticism. Umm, fur. Furry fur. Ohh love fur, just love it.

BRUNETTE: But I don't have fur.

BLONDE: But you can grow it.

BRUNETTE: Only for you.

BLONDE: Oh no, only if you want it too, not just for me.

BRUNETTE: Ohhhh but I adore fur and I adore you and I adore you adoring my future fur. Do you really love me?

BLONDE: Ohh, insanely, blissfully! You are my paradise. It'll take me years to explore every little part of you.

BRUNETTE: And when you've seen everything?

BLONDE: I would have forgotten what I saw first, so I'd want to start the whole thing all over again and explore everything again, and then forget again and start again, forget and start, forget and start, forget, start, forget, start...

BRUNETTE: Do you think my body is subtle?

BLONDE: Do I think your body is subtle? Oh God, oh what a...oh, your body is so subtle it's like an Ingmar Bergman film.

> (Somewhere at this point HUBERT
> has entered, unnoticed by the
> two women. JEREMIAH has also
> abandoned his dead man's position.
> The two men stare at this unusual
> encounter, from the shadows)

BLONDE: You are "The Virgin Spring" in "The Naked Night." Your face is "The Face" of "Cries and Whispers." Your smile is all the "Smiles of a Summer Night." Your breasts are the "Ports of Call." And your unmentionable is sweeter than "Wild Strawberries." Oh, in there your body's truly sublime. It's like "The Silence," "The Touch," "The Shame," "The Hour of the Wolf"...

(The women are suddenly aware
of the men's presence. A lengthy
stare. Quite unexpectedly, HUBERT
has a screaming, jumping, frenzied
fit, whereby, without any warning,
he rushes for the women's hair
which he immediately pulls with
wild malicious gusto. The scared,
screaming women run out, chased
by the outraged HUBERT. JEREMIAH
just stares)

BLACKOUT

(African music)

SCENE SIX

JEREMIAH and HUBERT are having a
siesta, in a sitting position,
back to back.

HUBERT: Jose?

JEREMIAH: Si?

HUBERT: Jose-e?

JEREMIAH: Siiii?

HUBERT: Jose, I think I saw a grass-hoppair!

JEREMIAH: A grass-hoppair?

HUBERT: Si, Jose, a grass-hoppair!

JEREMIAH: Where did you see a grass-hoppair,Juan?

HUBERT: On my nose, Juan!

JEREMIAH: Ah Juan, you are dreaming again.

HUBERT: No Jose, I am wide awake.

JEREMIAH: You are dreaming, Juan. There are no
grass-hoppairs here.

HUBERT: Si Jose. There is one.

JEREMIAH: And do you know where it is now, Juan?

HUBERT: Si Jose.

JEREMIAH: Where Juan?

HUBERT: I am not telling you, Jose.

JEREMIAH: Why not Juan?

HUBERT: Because you will steal it, Jose.

JEREMIAH: No Juan, I will not steal it.

HUBERT: Si Jose, you will steal it.

JEREMIAH: But I am not a thief, Juan.

HUBERT: No Jose?

JEREMIAH: No Juan. You know I am not.

HUBERT: Ah, maybe not, Jose, maybe not, but you
are one muchos grande bandido!

> (Both suddenly whirl around
> and angrily face each other.
> JEREMIAH doesn't like this.
> Not one bit. Daredevil
> HUBERT, however, looks danger-
> ously self-confident)

BLONDE: (Offstage, sing-song) I caught a grass-hopper, I caught a grasshopper.

JEREMIAH: (Angrily resuming his dead man's position) This is getting on my nerves. (To HUBERT) Bandido huh?

> (HUBERT, who has been saved in the nick of time, is now solely concerned with this latest development regarding the grass-hopper)

BLONDE: (Rushing in excitedly) I caught a grass-hopper, I caught a grasshopper.

HUBERT: (Chasing her angrily) You also have my car keys. Give me back my car keys. (BLONDE runs out) Hey, you come back here, I wanna see my grasshopper.

BRUNETTE: (Rushing in excitedly, Shirley Temple full blast) I caught a grasshopper, I caught a grasshopper, I caught a grasshopper. (HUBERT looks forlorn and defeated. BRUNETTE softens) Ohhhh! Hey, you wanna see my grasshopper?

HUBERT: (Jackie Coogan) That's not your grass-hopper, that's my grasshopper.

BRUNETTE: It is not. It's mine.

HUBERT: I tell you it's mine.

BRUNETTE: No, mine, mine, mine, mine, mine!

HUBERT: (Taking out gun) That insect belongs to me.

BRUNETTE: (Hands up) Ahhh, don't shoot!

HUBERT: Give it here.

BRUNETTE: Okay. But this is a present from me
to you.

> (HUBERT takes the grasshopper
> in his fist and has a peek at
> it. The BRUNETTE would like
> a peek too, but he doesn't
> let her. He then throws the
> invisible grasshopper up in
> the air and puts a bullet
> right through its privates)

HUBERT: (Laughing stupidly) Bull's Eye! Right
through its privates!

> (HUBERT has proved himself.
> The BRUNETTE is all goo-goo
> with amazement)

BRUNETTE: Hey, wanna fuck me?

HUBERT: Mind your own business.

BRUNETTE: Ah come on, fuck me.

HUBERT: Hit the road, kid.

BRUNETTE: Ah come on.

HUBERT: No.

BRUNETTE: Why not?

HUBERT·: Because.

BRUNETTE: Aw, that's no reason.

HUBERT: Sure it is.

BRUNETTE: It is not.

HUBERT: Is so.

BRUNETTE: Is not.

HUBERT: Is.

BRUNETTE: Not.

HUBERT: Is.

BRUNETTE: Not.

HUBERT: Is.

BRUNETTE: Not.

HUBERT: Is.

BRUNETTE: Oh yeah?

HUBERT: Yeah.

BRUNETTE: Oh yeah?

HUBERT: (Loud) Yeah.

BRUNETTE: (Louder) Oh yeah?

HUBERT: (Loudest) Yeaaaahhh!

BRUNETTE: (Whimpering) Ohhh!

HUBERT: (Feeling apologetic) I'm fussy.

BRUNETTE: So?

HUBERT: So that's my reason.

> (The BLONDE sticks her head
> in, sticks her tongue out
> at HUBERT, makes some funny
> phtt-sounding noises, and
> yanks out the BRUNETTE,
> claiming her for herself)

HUBERT: (Immediately yanking the BRUNETTE back in) Hey, come back here, I changed my mind.

BLONDE: That's not fair, it's not fair, not fair, you can't change your mind just like that.

JEREMIAH: (Abandoning his position) I can't stand this any longer.

HUBERT: Hey, you, lie down, you're dead.

BLONDE: (Frenzied excitement, to JEREMIAH) Aristotle!

BRUNETTE: (To JEREMIAH) Hey, I want an elephant.

JEREMIAH: (To BRUNETTE) Shut up kid.

BLONDE: Oh Aristotle, oh Ari, it's you, I found you, I found you at last, oh, Ari, I'm so happy. (Jumps on JEREMIAH's back and straddles him) Oh Ari, take me to the sea, ohhh I just gotta see the ocean once more before I die, the sea, Ari, the sea.

JEREMIAH: I can't help it, I'm just a sucker for blondes. (To HUBERT) See ya, gringo.

HUBERT: Yeah.

BRUNETTE: Hey, watch out for that swamp.

> (Exit JEREMIAH and the BLONDE.
> The BRUNETTE giggles at HUBERT.
> They are finally alone.
> HUBERT looks tough, cool and
> steely. He's Top Dog.
> The BRUNETTE is flustered.
> Cool jazz music.
> HUBERT goes downstage left, and
> faces the audience with his
> tough, cool, steely look.

He takes out a pack of Lucky
Strikes and cooly puts one in
the corner of his mouth. He
lights it cooly, with a cool
lighter.
The BRUNETTE now dons a new
image. The tough gal. She
goes downstage right, and faces
the audience with her tough gal
look. She's been around, she
knows the ropes, but she can't
fully hide that inner desolation
clawing at her heart. It's been
tough.
Music continues. HUBERT ignores
her)

BRUNETTE: Hey, gimme a puffer. (A lengthy stare)

HUBERT: (Snickering) Sure babe.

(HUBERT walks over to her, looking
tough, cool and steely. He produces his pack of Luckies with one
hand, and with the same hand, pats
the top of the pack, very coolly.
Three cigarettes fly out of the
pack and land on the ground.
HUBERT maintains his cool and pats
it again. Another three cigarettes
fly out and land on the ground.
Looking cooler than ever, he pats
again. The last three cigarettes
fly out and land on the ground.
HUBERT, coolness oozing out of
every pore, shakes the pack. Empty.
The BRUNETTE snickers.
HUBERT coolly flings the pack over
his shoulder and places his own lit
cigarette in her mouth, then coolly
walks over to his corner and coolly
produces a solitary cigarette from

                    a pocket and coolly lights it
                    and coolly smokes it. Both
                    smoke. Both look tough and
                    cool. The music slowly fades)

BRUNETTE: I wanna ask you a few questions about
last Friday.

HUBERT: She had a beauty spot right here. (Meaning
the thigh)

BRUNETTE: Maybe you should stop seeing me right
now.

HUBERT: (Snicker) It don't have nothing to do
with you, babe.

BRUNETTE: All those dates I've had to break, and
for what? (Cough)

HUBERT: (Snicker) Listen, babe, you wanna stop
seeing me, that's okay with me.

BRUNETTE: (Fatal) Maybe... (Takes a step to
him) Maybe, I just want you to tell me that you
love me.

HUBERT: (Cool) I love you...stupid.

BRUNETTE: (Fatal) Ohh! Look, I'm a girl and
I'm good.

HUBERT: (Takes a cool step forward) So?

BRUNETTE: So that's two out of three.

HUBERT: (Takes another cool step) So?

BRUNETTE: So you got stars in your eyes and I put
'em there, not her.

HUBERT: (Another cool step) So?

BRUNETTE: (Angrily stomping out her cigarette)
So you shouldn't have done that. You shouldn't
have kissed her.

HUBERT: (Snicker) So? (Turns his back on her)

BRUNETTE: (Snatching his gun from his pocket)
So I'll remember to the end of my life that there
are men like you alive. (A tense moment, as the
BRUNETTE points the gun at HUBERT's heart. HUBERT
is cool) Ohh, I can't do it.

> (HUBERT snickers. HUBERT coolly
> stamps out his cigarette. HUBERT
> coolly stretches out his hand.
> HUBERT coolly waits. The BRUNETTE
> fatally relinquishes the gun.
> HUBERT coolly pockets it. HUBERT
> coolly takes a step forward.
> HUBERT coolly gives the BRUNETTE
> three quick stinging slaps on her
> face. BRUNETTE whimpers)

BRUNETTE: Ohhh! You big bully!

> (HUBERT coolly puts his arm around
> her waist, and coolly pulls her to
> him and coolly gives her a brutally
> passionate kiss, fully on the lips.
> BRUNETTE melting very fast, to
> audience)

BRUNETTE: Ohhh! It's a lousy game.

BLACKOUT

(Cool James Bond music)

THE END

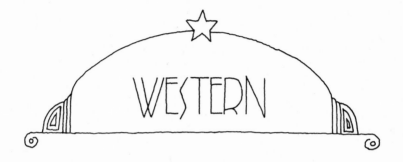

WESTERN

Arizona, 1874

Three stage-coach travellers, ambushed by 500
hostile Indians, have managed to hide behind
some rocks up in the hills:

BART, a yet untested gunfighter,

LILI, a pampered Eastern Belle,

JEAN, a tough farmer's daughter.

Below, "the 500" wait.

Tense music heightens the immediacy of the
moment.

SCENE ONE

(A long pause)

LILI: (Peeping from behind a rock, terrified)
Apache.

JEAN: (Composed, she's had a few ambushes in
her time) Burt Lancaster.

LILI: (Keeping up the terror) Apache Territory.

JEAN: (Definite scorn for the East) Rory
Calhoun.

LILI: (Hearing something) Apache Drums.

JEAN: (A confirmation) Stephen McNally.

LILI: (Seeing something) Apache War Smoke.

JEAN: (Another confirmation) Gilbert Roland.

LILI: (Realizing something) Apache Ambush.

JEAN: (Yet another confirmation, but No Big
Deal) Bill Williams.

LILI: (Hysterical) Geronimo.

JEAN: (Putting her foot down) Chuck Connors.

(Pause. An arrow whizzes past her)

JEAN: (Shaken) War Arrow.

LILI: (Beyond hysteria) Jeff Chandler.

JEAN: (Weak) Blood Arrow.

LILI: (Far gone) Scott Brady.

(Pause)

LILI: (Hopelessly helpless, now turns to the inconspicuous BART, his sex being fully considered and found very suitable for the task at hand) Colt 45.

BART: (Cautious) Randolph Scott.

LILI: (Hysterically challenging his manhood) Springfield Rifle.

BART: (Undaunted) Gary Cooper.

LILI: (A deliberate intimidation, with more than a tone of doubt regarding his virility) Winchester 73.

BART: (Too smart to fall into the devious trap) James Stewart.

LILI: (A last whimpering plea) Winchester 73. Remake.

BART: (Smartly vigilant) Tom Tyron.

(Pause)

JEAN: (Smarter than she looks. Decides to use the poetic approach) Gun Fury.

BART: (He surprises the ladies with his unexpected enthusiasm, fully revealing his weak spot in the process) Rock Hudson.

JEAN: (Jumps on him) Gun Glory.

BART: (Belligerently zealous) Stewart Granger.

JEAN: (Pounces) Gun The Man Down.

BART: (Sweepingly vehement) James Arness.

JEAN: (Reverently solemn) Top Gun.

BART: (Impetuously intense) Sterling Hayden.

       (Pause)

LILI: (Easy bait now) The Searchers.

BART: (Mellifluous poetry) John Wayne.

JEAN: (Urging him to heights, the way only a woman can) The Comancheros.

BART: (An enviously unattainable goal) John Wayne.

LILI: (Desperate for a hero) The Horse Soldiers.

BART: (Maybe it's worth a try) John Wayne.

JEAN: (Lest we forget) The Alamo.

BART: (Damn well worth a try) John Wayne.

LILI: (What more can she say?) The Cowboys.

BART: (This is it, he's gonna go) John Wayne.

JEAN: (One last one for the road) The Undefeated.

BART: (Duck, you suckers!) Big! John! Wayne!

                  (Daredevil BART demonstrates
                  a quick draw and several un-
                  deniably striking poses. Pro-
                  ducing a cigar, he then sizes
                  up the situation, emits a
                  "Yup" and exits defiantly with
                  blazing guns. Pause. Silence.
                  A man screams out, twice)

JEAN: (Distressed) Shane.

LILI: (Equally distressed) Shane.

JEAN: (More distressed) Shane.

LILI: (Equally more distressed) Shane.

JEAN: (Panicky) Shane.

LILI: (Equally panicky) Shane.

　　　　　(JEAN, now having convinced
　　　　　herself that BART is in danger,
　　　　　decides to bravely go out and
　　　　　help. LILI, scared to remain
　　　　　alone, struggles to keep JEAN
　　　　　back. JEAN knocks out LILI's
　　　　　front teeth with her rifle
　　　　　butt and exits)

　　　　　　　　　BLACKOUT

　　　　　(A jovial square dance is heard
　　　　　during the BLACKOUT. Equally
　　　　　whirling music is heard during
　　　　　all subsequent blackouts)

　　　　　　　　SCENE TWO

　　　　　(Courageous BART is back. LILI
　　　　　is showing him her leg)

LILI: (A flutter of eyelids) True Grit.

BART: (Feeling Top Dog) John Wayne.

LILI: (More flutters) Tall In The Saddle.

BART: (Even Topper Dog) John Wayne.

　　　　　(A woman screams out)
128

LILI: (Reluctant to give up her pursuit) The Indian Fighter.

BART: (Worried about the scream) Kirk Douglas.

LILI: (Blind to her preoccupation) Man Of The West.

BART: (Still worried) Gary Cooper.

LILI: (Blatantly passionate) Only The Valient.

BART: (Her charms beginning to work on him) Gregory Peck.

> (The woman screams again. BART takes a second to think and decides to go and help. Scared LILI clings to him, refusing to let him go. Frenzied BART shoots her hand off and exits)

BLACKOUT

SCENE THREE

> (Valiant BART now with grateful JEAN)

JEAN: (A trifle uneasy now, suggests possible centres of refuge to stubborn BART) Fort Apache ... Fort Dobbs... Fort Worth... Fort Yuma...

(A woman screams)

BART: (Slapped back to reality by the agonized tone of the scream) She Wore A Yellow Ribbon.

(BART decides to go and help. Jealous
JEAN struggles to keep him back. JEAN
is knocked down with a punch in the
face. BART exits)

BLACKOUT

SCENE FOUR

(JEAN and LILI have somehow come
across each other. They are hiding.
They don't have too much to say.
A man screams out)

JEAN: (Delirious) My Darling Clementine.

(JEAN frenziedly rushes out to help
but not before LILI gets to her. A
fight. LILI gets knocked down. She
quickly grabs her gun and shoots JEAN
in the back. JEAN falls dead)

BLACKOUT

SCENE FIVE

(BART and LILI reunited. BART is
aware of a missing JEAN)

BART: (Inquisitive) Cat Ballou.

LILI: (Cool) The Scalp Hunters.

BART: (Not convinced) Cat Ballou...Cat Ballou...

                    (BART is about to go and look for
                    her)

LILI: (Sombre, despite herself) Death Of A
Gunfighter.

                    (BART stops dead in his tracks. A
                    silent moment)

                         BLACKOUT

                         SCENE SIX

                    (BART and LILI again. BART still
                    looking for Indians. LILI looking
                    for love. Panting, passionate LILI
                    is determined. BART is still pre-
                    occupied. Wanton LILI forcefully
                    kisses helpless BART. An unending
                    kiss. Revived JEAN creeps in un-
                    noticed, and does not like what she
                    sees. She noisily cocks her gun
                    and shoots the alarmed LILI in the
                    face. LILI falls dead in BART's lap)

JEAN: The Stranger Returns.

                         BLACKOUT

                         SCENE SEVEN

                    (BART and JEAN now. Alert BART

looking for Indians. JEAN looking
for love. Tactless JEAN is ignored
by preoccupied BART. No-nonsense
JEAN offers some friendly persuasion.
Helpless BART feels the pointed gun
and decides not to argue. Brazen
JEAN forcefully kisses BART. An
equally lengthy kiss. Revived LILI
walks in with determined eyes. She
kicks JEAN out of position and fires
her gun right in between BART's eyes.
BART's death is quick)

LILI: Last of the Fast Guns.

                    BLACKOUT

                    SCENE EIGHT

(JEAN and LILI with piercing glares.
Flared passions are admirably controlled. Revived BART enters with a
broad smile. A contagious smile.
For a moment all is forgiven. But not
for long. BART shoots LILI in the
guts. BART shoots JEAN in the neck.
JEAN's death is instantaneous, but
LILI refuses to die, becoming very
noisy in the process. BART blasts
her brains out. LILI dies mercifully.
Nonchalant BART holsters his gun with
satisfaction)

BART: They Died With Their Boots On.

                    BLACKOUT

132

SCENE NINE

(BART, LILI, JEAN. Hiding. Looking
for Indians. BART shaking, LILI
sobbing, JEAN starting. Three shots.
Lengthy contortions. Heart-rending
screams. BART got it in the guts,
LILI in the forehead, JEAN in the
back. After all three are dead, a
hollow voice is heard)

VOICE: High Noon.

BLACKOUT

SCENE TEN

(No one. Silence. In the distance,
ten Cavalry calls are heard, as the
columns rush to do their duty)

BLACKOUT

(The music comes to a Grand Finale)

THE END

CHRISTMAS

THE PLACE:

Anywhere.

THE TIME:

The Present.

THE SET:

Three Black Walls.

A Christmas Holly Wreath hung on the
upstage wall.

A small table.

A chair or two.

THE LENGTH OF THE PLAY:

Thirty minutes.

CHARACTERS AND COSTUMES

THE CHRISTMAS TREE.....Green pants, green T-shirt,
               green socks, brown shoes.

THE LUMBERJACK.....Ordinary dress, preferably in
          faded blues and greys.

THE YOUNG MAN.....Ordinary dress, conservative,
          subdued. A coat, a little worn-out.

THE YOUNG WOMAN.....Ordinary dress, conservative,
          subdued.   A little worn-out.

THE DOG.....Plain pants, heavy sweater, bare feet.

THE VIOLINIST/PIANIST.....Offstage.

GENERAL NOTES

This is a play without any dialogue. It is not a
mime play. In fact, the use of mime, in all its
aspects should be avoided altogether. However,
objects and activities could be indicated if
necessary.

This play, like any other ordinary dialogue play,
is basically dependent on language as a means of
communication. Consequently the characters in
the play relate to each other very simply, by
talking. However, not one single word or whisper
may be heard.

The actors should, during rehearsals, improvise
and set certain dialogue to guide them through
the play, or use the dialogue provided sporadic-
ally in the text, then mouth them out in total
silence during performances, hence creating a
very naturalistic style.

The CHRISTMAS TREE is played throughout as a very
human character, no different. The only thing
odd about him should be the fact that his feet
are stuck to the ground in the first scene.

The DOG is played as what it is. He or she walks
on all fours and has all the characteristics of a
dog.

NOTES ON THE MUSIC

Music is essential to this play.

Prior to the performance, there should be audience music consisting of various familiar Christmas carols.

There is a continuous musical accompaniment throughout the play (solo violin or solo piano), except where otherwise stated.

The music should be live.

The violinist or pianist should play from a backstage area and should not be visible to the audience.

Unless otherwise specified, the music should mainly be improvised in accordance with the action onstage, heightening dramatic moments when necessary and otherwise setting the mood, much like the musical accompaniment to early silent films.

No modern tunes may be played, the general nature of the music being snatches of classical pieces, Christmas carols, or on the spot improvised mood setters.

In Scene Four, a single brooding bass chord should be played repeatedly all throughout at a constant beat of a count of four, and at a constant volume. If a piano is unavailable, the same effect should be duplicated on the violin.

In Scene Five, the music should be Schubert's "Ave Maria".

SCENE ONE

Music: "Silent Night"

The Wide Open.
Christmas Eve.
Peaceful. Cold. Snow.

A solitary CHRISTMAS TREE stands, asleep in the
open. Immobile, hands sheltering shoulders,
drooping head, eyes closed.

Lengthy pause.

The CHRISTMAS TREE gradually wakes from his sleep.
Stretching langorously, he suddenly feels the
sharp sting of the cold. Not stopping to think,
he instantly hurls himself into a flurry of rapid
motion, trying to rub some warmth into his body.

Of course his feet are solidly planted in the
ground, and try what he may, he simply cannot get
himself unstuck. Several futile efforts later,
he finally resigns himself to his fate and tries
to make the best of his situation by continuing
his constant state of mobility.

What a life, what a life!

When suddenly a LUMBERJACK appears out of nowhere
and commences to stare most intently at the
CHRISTMAS TREE. The LUMBERJACK has an axe flung
over his shoulder.

The CHRISTMAS TREE notices him. Hi, hello, how
are you? No reply. The CHRISTMAS TREE, however,
does not give up. A spot of friendly conversation
is hard to find in these here parts. Nasty
weather, isn't it Sir? Yes, very nasty, even if
you don't say so yourself. Sorry, can't shake
your hand Sir. Can't stretch out that far.

You see, I'm sort of stuck. Now isn't that ridiculous, ho-ho? Is that what you were just thinking. Can't hear you Sir! Oh, you didn't say nothing. I see.

The LUMBERJACK, an unfriendly sort, ignores his conversation and concentrates on a meticulous inspection of the whole length of his trunk.

The CHRISTMAS TREE notices the LUMBERJACK'S curious new interest and becomes a trifle uneasy. Genuine solid one hundred percent bark, Sir. Very expensive, but what the hell, you only live once, right Sir?

The LUMBERJACK slowly circles around him. You wouldn't buy any chance be a connoisseur of bark, would...

When without any warning the LUMBERJACK swings his axe and strikes the CHRISTMAS TREE at the bottom of his trunk, repeatedly felling the CHRISTMAS TREE at the ankles, watching him gradually lose his balance as he silently administers an unending flurry of chops.

The alarmed CHRISTMAS TREE, stung by the pain of these unexpected blows and totally powerless to stop the unrelenting axe, doesn't even have time to think before he suddenly finds himself face down on the ground.

All civility gone, he angrily gets up, roughly grabs the frightened LUMBERJACK and is about to punch him in the face, when he notices the frantic LUMBERJACK wildly gesticulating at his feet.

By golly, he's right! I didn't realize this! I can walk! I·can walk!

Dropping the LUMBERJACK, he celebrates his new-found freedom by merrily tap-dancing all over the place. He rushes to the bewildered LUMBERJACK, gratefully gives him a bear hug, almost succeeding in crushing all his ribs, then throwing him aside, he shouts his thanks to the heavens, then grabs the dizzy LUMBERJACK once more and indulges in some furious rock 'n' roll as he basks in his new-found glory. Once again the hapless LUMBERJACK finds himself hurled into a summersault. At this point he thinks best to make a getaway and noticing the CHRISTMAS TREE has his back turned he commences to tip-toe out, when he suddenly finds himself yanked back by the scruff of his neck.

Not so fast, not so fast kid. Now you ain't thinking of deserting me are you? No Sir, no Sir, no, of course not. Well, I'm glad to hear that, because you realize you have a responsibility now! Responsibility? Why sure, kid, now that you've got me chopped, you've got to get me sold, right? But, but, but. A-a, no buts, it's all part of the job. But I'm no salesman, Mr. Tree. Ah come, come, you can't fool me. Under every LUMBERJACK, there's a salesman just dying to come and be heard. But I assure you Mr. Tree... Mr. Lumberjack, please don't be difficult!

The CHRISTMAS TREE'S friendly persuasion seems to take effect, and as luck would have it, at that precise moment they notice their prospective customer: a young man, who seems to be rather out on his luck, cheerlessly inspecting the inflationary price tags on some imaginary Christmas trees.

The CHRISTMAS TREE prods the reluctant LUMBERJACK forward. Now there's your chance mac, there's a live one for you, you can't miss. Now show us that super-duper salesmanship of yours in action. C'mon kid, what are you waiting for. Go on, dum-

dum, grab the guy. The nervous, confused
LUMBERJACK hesitantly goes over to the young man,
and mumbles a few unintelligible sounds to him.
Never before, has any one blown a deal so
totally, so effortlessly.

The CHRISTMAS TREE realizing his mistake,
quickly steps in. Unceremoniously pushing the
LUMBERJACK aside, he puts on his toothy million
dollar smile, instantly shrouds the YOUNG MAN
with his magnetic charm, and chummily commences
to describe to him, with a friendly arm on his
shoulder, of course, why he couldn't possibly
refuse his offer.

One thing the CHRISTMAS TREE ain't, however, is a
good bargainer. He cheerfully lets the price
drop and drop and drop... Wait a minute now,
interjects Mr. Lumberjack, I may be stupid, but I
ain't that stupid. Be quiet, replies the
CHRISTMAS TREE, as he closes his trap for him,
after all, it's only money, right Sir? The YOUNG
MAN agrees, as he drops the price a little more.
Whatever you say Sir, only we're wasting time
here, it's rather cold you know. What say you we
wrap up this deal?

My final offer... Done! Highway robbery,
comments the LUMBERJACK. You know something, you
got a big mouth. Taking the money the YOUNG MAN
offers, the CHRISTMAS TREE shoves it in his...
fist. You don't like violence Sir? Oh neither
do I, no Sir. Lucky ding-a-ling. Well, thank you
for everything, good-bye, and kicks the LUMBER-
JACK off. Nearly blew this deal, the dumb jerk.

Well Sir, shall we be on our way now? And so they
happily depart for home, the CHRISTMAS TREE
assuring the YOUNG MAN that he has made a terrific
bargain. Yes siree, 'cause you don't realize
this, but I'm gonna make this Christmas, the
happiest, merriest Christmas you'll ever have.

'Cause that's my game Sir, to bring that good ol'
Christmas cheer to your lovely little home. Ah
Christmas, now I really start to live.

And the two friends merrily go on their way.

BLACKOUT

Music continues in black.

SCENE TWO

The YOUNG MAN'S home.
Poorly furnished.

The YOUNG WOMAN, the YOUNG MAN'S wife, an
innocent young thing, is seated with a bundle of
newspapers on her lap, day-dreaming. She is a
trifle sad because they're so poor. She dreams
of the joys of having a nice big CHRISTMAS TREE
and colourful Christmas decorations and all those
other nice Christmassy things. She sighs
resignedly as she glances at the newspapers and
sadly resumes cutting more doll-shaped designs,
the only Christmas decoration they can afford.

When in comes HUBBY. Hello Sweetheart! Hello
Darling! WIFEY tenderly welcomes HUBBY home as
they cuddle up contentedly for a kiss. Had a
nice day? What did you do? WIFEY points out the
decorations that she'd been making. HUBBY
expresses his delight. Beautiful, just beautiful.
I've made some more, they're in the kitchen, I'll
show them to you. WIFEY rushes off excitedly to
the kitchen.

Taking this opportune moment, HUBBY signals the
hidden CHRISTMAS TREE to enter. The CHRISTMAS
TREE sneaks in, brimming with excitement, but

144

also a little shy. So this is home, sweet home.
I love it. Just love it. It's so warm in here.
Now, now, hush, Mr. Tree, I want you to be a big
surprise for my wife. Yes, of course, I understand, this is very exciting. HUBBY fusses over
the CHRISTMAS TREE, dusting his T-shirt, making
sure his eye-brows are combed, a million other
things. The CHRISTMAS TREE, meek, but with a
mischievous glint in his eye, slowly reversing
the situation by fussing over HUBBY in return.

Confusion! Excitement! Finally they're ready!
Both strike chivalrous poses in eager anticipation
of WIFEY'S big return.

WIFEY enters with several strings of popcorn
suddenly starts as she sees the CHRISTMAS TREE.
This is indeed a surprise! A long, tense minute
of silence from all three. Indeed, she's so
surprised, that she seems to be rooted in her
open-mouthed, stunned gape. HUBBY and the
CHRISTMAS TREE begin to feel a trifle uncomfortable.
The everpresent question is: Have we disappointed
her? No, that's not possible, thinks the
CHRISTMAS TREE as he heaves out his chest an
extra inch and puts some more sparkle on that
toothy smile of his. Still the same immobile
gaze. The CHRISTMAS TREE is stunned. Well,
obviously I've failed, she is not impressed.
Manfully taking all the blame on himself, he sees
no alternative but to leave.

When WIFEY explodes onto HUBBY with a profusion
of tearful thanks. She apologizes for her
behaviour, explaining that she had been jolted
into an extreme state of happiness, for she had
most certainly not expected something as
extravagant as a CHRISTMAS TREE, the only thing
she truly desired. Oh how did he guess that was
what she wanted?

And so showering her gratitude on the happy but
also a little embarrassed HUBBY, she rejoices at
the prospect of a very merry Christmas indeed.

The CHRISTMAS TREE, having been transfixed in a
highly emotional state all this while, can feel
his knees giving out as WIFEY demurely approaches
him, and sincerely expresses how honoured she is
at having him as a Christmas guest. The CHRISTMAS
TREE threatens to cry with joy, when HUBBY loudly
interjects and announces that it's now CHRISTMAS
TREE decorating time.

All quickly agree and prance around with joy,
WIFEY quickly darts out into the kitchen and darts
back in with more popcorn and a couple of socks.
Why the socks, wonders the CHRISTMAS TREE.

I did these all by myself, aren't they nice! she
exclaims. All agree that the strings of popcorn
are indeed delightful works of art. But then,
lo and behold, WIFEY commences to wrap the strings
around the bewildered CHRISTMAS TREE. Bracelets
of popcorn! A popcorn belt! A popcorn crown!
What, what, what's going on here! We're
decorating you, Mr. Christmas Tree. Methinks,
thinks the CHRISTMAS TREE, now this is a different
matter. Now, excuse me lady, but permit me to
explain... will you hold for a minute please!
Now the definition of CHRISTMAS TREE decorations
is, and he nicely puts his foot down, nicely but
firmly, pointing out to the over-excited couple
that popcorn and Christmas Trees don't exactly
mix. Cheerfully undaunted, WIFEY, however, has
her own ideas about decorating and begs to differ.
Why popcorn goes so well with you, Mr. Tree!
HUBBY blindly agrees, and both busily bombard the
poor CHRISTMAS TREE with tons of popcorn.

The CHRISTMAS TREE looks out morosely and
meditates on the inevitability of fate. But this
is stupid! I mean it's stupid! I look stupid,

the whole idea is stupid, the very thought is
stupid, boy oh boy! But wait a minute, what's
this? I see light bulbs! Aloha, an idea! He
does a little Hawaiian dance to point out how
ridiculous he must look with popcorn all over him.
The couple's reply is a frenzy of applause, as
they cheer for more. They didn't get the message!

Well, this is it, I didn't want to do this, but I
guess I'll have to. The CHRISTMAS TREE sweetly
but sternly tells the couple that popcorn is
definitely out. I'm very sorry, but it just will
not do. And he commences to remove it, string
by string. He nicely explains to them that a nice
set of clothes will do just fine and dandy. Just
lemme try them on, they'll look far better on me,
I promise you.

The couple are disappointed and far from convinced.
They make one more attempt to string him with
popcorn. An abortive attempt. Especially since
this time around, they decided to include the
socks. The CHRISTMAS TREE is not amused. In
fact, removing a sock from the top of his nose, he
becomes downright stubborn. I want clothes or I
stay the way I am, and voila that is my ultimatum!

HUBBY, a trifle amused at the CHRISTMAS TREE's
obstinacy, decides to go along with him, urging
WIFEY to give it a try as well. WIFEY argues.
HUBBY sweetly implores. WIFEY softens and goes
off to fetch the desired objects, but not without
first giving them both a piece of her mind. The
CHRISTMAS TREE commends HUBBY on his good sense
and assures him that: I know what I'm doing.
When WIFEY enters, muttering her discontent, and
presents the tree, not too ceremoniously with a
multicoloured vest, a multicoloured tie and a
multicoloured ski cap.

Oh well, sighs the CHRISTMAS TREE, I suppose
they'll have to do. No, no, I'm not being picky.
They'll do just fine, no really, I love them.
I was only kidding. Honest. Terrific threads
these. And indeed they are, for the CHRISTMAS
TREE puts on the tie, and there it is for all to
see. The colour combinations are so exquisitely
right, so poignantly delightful against his green
T-shirt, that the couple are speedily convinced
of their previous error in judgement. Indeed,
WIFEY is so delighted that she insists on
dressing him herself and gustily commences to
twist the CHRISTMAS TREE'S arms to accommodate
the vest. HUBBY joining in as well, not exactly
knowing what to do, but joining in anyway. The
CHRISTMAS TREE politely asks for permission to do
it himself. WIFEY refuses as she cheerfully
battles with a button.

And so amidst much confusion, excitement and good
cheer, they finally manage to get the poor
CHRISTMAS TREE fully dressed and decorated. The
CHRISTMAS TREE acquires the privilege of putting
the finishing touches on the cap himself as the
couple stand aside to gaze on the object of their
toil. A silence envelops the room. The
CHRISTMAS TREE quizzically turns to see if anything's the matter and is quite surprised by the
look on their faces... for all the couple can do
is stand gaping at him with serene child-like
wonder, breathlessly marvelling at his
transformation. Ohhhh, Christmas Tree, you're
so beautiful!

The CHRISTMAS TREE, a very modest tree, feels a
trifle self-conscious: Oh come, come, surely you
exaggerate. Drawing himself to his full length,
however, he can't resist showing off a little.
The CHRISTMAS TREE is very happy indeed, for he
knows only too well that this is what he was made
for, and now at long last he has aspired to his
true purpose in life, to spread the blessed
Christmas joy to one and all.

148

The CHRISTMAS TREE then has a little idea and says
that everything would truly be perfect if he only
had a multicoloured coat as well. Yes, I think
what I need is just a teeny-weeny extra oomph,
and then I've really got it made. Yeah, I mean,
then, I've really made it. What do ya say kids?

The couple suddenly become very downcast and try
to avoid his eyes. What's the matter? Did I say
something wrong? HUBBY sadly confesses that much
as they would like to oblige, their current
economic plight will not allow them to provide him
with that necessity.

The CHRISTMAS TREE angrily smacks his head as he
realizes the gigantic boo-boo he just committed.
He quickly assures the couple that his desire is
far from a necessity. A mere luxury, honest, no
I mean really, who needs a coat, I mean what will
I do with it, I ain't planning on going anywhere.
Look, just forget it, o.k., no really, I feel top
of the world in this outfit. Come to think of it,
a coat would ruin the overall effect. Yeah, why
didn't I think of that before. Listen, I'm
telling you, even if you did get me a coat now, I
wouldn't wear it. Who needs it, I'm beautiful as
it is, right?

The couple try to be convinced but aren't, too
many nasty thoughts popping up now, HUBBY jobless,
their money running out, what does the future have
in store for them... what indeed?

The CHRISTMAS TREE immediately interjects. This
situation is beginning to get out of hand, I
better do something about it, and gently
admonishes the couple: Now these are not very
nice Christmas thoughts. Shame on you. This is
a time for cheer and merriment. This is also a
time for sacred holy thoughts. Now I don't see
you doing either of these. Money! Now you tell
me, is it proper to think about something like

that on Christmas Eve? Don't worry, you ain't
gonna starve, tomorrow is another day, and
tomorrow is sure to have a lot of good things in
mind just for the two of you. Come, come, now,
you worry too much. Think of the things you
already have, and lemme tell you this, you can
count yourselves lucky, 'cause a lot of people
ain't got as much. You're both healthy, you got
a roof over your heads, you got enough bread on
the table to last you for quite a few days, and
most important of all, you got each other and
you're in love. Now what's more important than
that?

These words of wisdom make their impact felt.
The couple realize how foolish they were to worry
about little things like that at an important
time like this and they're quickly cheered again,
especially when they look into each other's eyes
and find an affirmation of their love.

The CHRISTMAS TREE hoofs a couple of steps.
Everyone is amused, all nasty thoughts are
forgotten, and the Christmas spirit is now
securely lodged in everyone's heart, thanks to the
delightful CHRISTMAS TREE.

Yes, siree, they're gonna have a very merry
Christmas indeed.

BLACKOUT

SCENE THREE

The Couple's home.

Early Christmas morn. A few minutes past
midnight.

150

The CHRISTMAS TREE is cheerfully arranging the
two presents he has for the couple. He fusses
for an eternity over them, finally settling on the
perfect position and the perfect angle to lay them
down. He then darts out and darts back in with
a couple of Christmas crackers and spends another
eternity arranging those. Brimming with merriment
he makes sure that everything is neat and tidy
and all ready for the couple's return. He
interjects his house-keeping with frequent peeks
out the window.

Finally everything is all set. Pacing about,
peeking more often out the window now, he awaits
the return of the two, when he suddenly hears
some footsteps in the hallway. He zooms to a spot
behind where the presents have been set, and
putting on a big smile, he gets ready to greet
them with this big surprise. He tensely waits
for the door to unlock. No sound. Why are they
taking so long? Trouble with the key perhaps?
Still no sound! Better go and check, they might
have lost their key or something.

He sadly re-enters with drooping head. False
alarm, it wasn't them. Where on earth can they
be? More glances out the window. They're late.
Something's happened to them. An accident. No,
no, no, don't be silly. They're just taking their
time. It's a pleasant night out. They're
probably having a little stroll. And again maybe
they're not. Perhaps... perhaps they're not going
to come back. Oh, but that's impossible, why
would they do a silly thing like that? They have
to come back, if only so they can open their
presents. They'd surely want to open up their
presents, wouldn't they? Wouldn't anyone? But
then again maybe they don't believe in Santa Claus
any more. Oh that's ridiculous. Even if they
didn't, which I don't think is true, they'd still
want to open the presents they bought for each
other. Perhaps it's none of these things at all.

151

Perhaps they met some friends on the way and have decided to spend their Christmas somewhere else. No, no, no, out of the question.

Plagued by a thousand such thoughts, the CHRISTMAS TREE grows increasingly nervous and begins to feel very lonely. One long look out the window reveals them to be nowhere in sight.

Sadly he goes and takes a seat and tries to distract himself by looking at the presents. He looks at them tenderly as he feels them, trying to guess their contents. This makes him even sadder. Sad at the thought of them not coming home to open their presents. Why are they so late? Where can they be at this hour of the night? Midnight Mass has been over for some time now.

Finally the truth strikes home. There is no other possible explanation. Evidently they had been invited out previously and had forgotten to tell him about it. They're probably at their friends' house right now, celebrating Christmas, having a lot of fun.

Then all my preparations were in vain, thinks the CHRISTMAS TREE. Imagine, waiting a lifetime so I can help a couple celebrate one Christmas, a whole lifetime for one blessed day, and they decide to be somewhere else. It's only this one day I'm asking them to be present here with me. Just for one day. Oh, why did they bother to buy me, if they weren't even gonna spend their Christmas at home. I'd have been much better off the way I was before, rooted in the snow... This is so cruel, letting me spend Christmas all alone, with no one to spread cheer to. Just left all by myself, unseen, forgotten... The CHRISTMAS TREE silently gazes at the presents, with moist eyes.

When suddenly the loudest of noises can be heard.
What the! The door. The key. The door's opened.
They're here. For a moment he's so confused he
doesn't know what to do, till he suddenly realizes:
they're back! Hurriedly drying his tears he just
barely manages to run to his position when in come
the couple, warmly greeting the CHRISTMAS TREE.
Hello Christmas Tree. Brrrr, it's cold outside,
and there weren't any buses, so we had to walk.
Oh, it's so nice to be back home. Oh I'm cold,
I'm cold.

The CHRISTMAS TREE is so relieved. Oh please let
me take your coats for you. You'll soon warm up.
Oh cold, cold, cold. Yes well, you'll soon be
warm. Cold, cold. Yes, ahem, I say, ahem. The
CHRISTMAS TREE politely asks to be heard. Ahem.
Yes, Christmas Tree? You wish to say something?
Eh, yes actually. There is a little surprise
waiting for you. Surprise? Where? Eh yes, over
there. If you just look over there, you'll notice
someone has paid you a visit while you were away.
No, no, over there. Right there. Yes! The
couple finally notices the presents. Santa Claus!
Oh Hooray! He remembered us.

They happily rush over to the presents as the
delighted CHRISTMAS TREE looks on. The couple are
about to grab their presents when they suddenly
pause for a minute. Looking tenderly into each
other's eyes, they embrace lovingly and wish each
other the merriest of Christmases.

Then they hand over their presents to one another.
From me to you. And like happy children they
settle down to begin the exquisite task of ripping
off the wrapping paper.

What's this? Oh how sweet! A scarf! Just what I
needed. Did you make this yourself? All by yourself? Oh my dearest, you shouldn't have. Oh thank
you, thank you so much.

Ohhhh! A pair of mittens! Oh my darling, thank you, thank you, thank you.

The CHRISTMAS TREE intrudes gently, before we all choke up, here is a little something from me to you, and meekly offers each a party cracker. One each. Merry Christmas.

This they had not expected. A present from a Christmas Tree? Why thank you, thank you so much. And they merrily pop a cracker. Hooray! I win! I win! On to the next, when WIFEY stops, deciding that the CHRISTMAS TREE should share this cracker. HUBBY agrees and urges WIFEY to go ahead. No, WIFEY says, you and the CHRISTMAS TREE. No, no, you. And the CHRISTMAS TREE says, no, no, no, it's for the two of you. No you. No you. No you. Until finally WIFEY goes over to the CHRISTMAS TREE and insists that he participate. Yes m'am. And HUBBY insists that she share it with the CHRISTMAS TREE. Yes sir. The CHRISTMAS TREE asks Hubby: but are you absolutely sure, I mean I don't want you to be left out. Please Mr Tree, do pop the cracker, won't you? Yes sir. And so at last the cracker is popped. Hooray! I win! I win! WIFEY jumps happily. I win! The CHRISTMAS TREE shyly pecks a tiny kiss on her cheek and then vehemently shakes HUBBY's hand saying how honoured he is to adorn their home and what a privilege that they should have chosen him out of a million other Christmas Trees.

WIFEY fondly returns the kiss and HUBBY warmly puts an arm around the CHRISTMAS TREE's shoulder, both insisting that it was only because of him that this Christmas has turned out to be the best and merriest Christmas they have ever had.

The grateful CHRISTMAS TREE finds himself beyond happiness. At last, my purpose in life finally achieved. I was able to make two people happy on this Holy Christmas Day. I am so glad! So glad.

The couple warmly smile at him with gratitude.
Thank you for making us happy.

The CHRISTMAS TREE is unable to hide his tears
any longer. It was my pleasure.

SLOW BLACKOUT

The music comes to a delicate finish.

SCENE FOUR

Music: None. Total silence.

The Couple's home.
The morning after New Year's.

The festivities are now over and life has returned
to normal.

WIFEY is seated in a corner, immersed in a serious
book. The CHRISTMAS TREE is wandering about
trying to think up some interesting activities to
occupy himself with. He looks out the window.
Nothing interesting. He looks around the room.
Nothing interesting. He looks at WIFEY. No
reaction. A little friendly cough. Still no
reaction. Some haphazard tap dancing. Boy, that
book must really be something. Ah, but it's boring
around here. He takes out a pack of cards for a
game of solitaire. Nah, that's a stupid game.
Besides I don't feel like it. I mean: What is a
Christmas Tree supposed to do after Christmas?
Well, I guess keep up that good ole Christmas
cheer. That's the only thing I'm good at anyway.
But I can't do it alone, I need some participation
from other folks as well. I wonder why no one's
interested in being merry anymore? There's no
law that says you can't, just 'cause Christmas is

155

over. Oh well, I mustn't give up. Gotta keep
trying. He stands on his head. Another friendly
cough. WIFEY looks. Smiles faintly at his
antics. Back to book. Well that's encouraging
anyway. The CHRISTMAS TREE gets up and goes over
to WIFEY. Feeling sprightly, sociable, he settles
down for a meaningful conversation on books.
WIFEY would really prefer to read, so she flashes
the occasional smile, but tries to concentrate on
the book. The CHRISTMAS TREE does not get the
message. Hmmm! Philosophy, you don't say. Well,
well, well. May I just look at the cover for a
moment please. Aristotle! Oh yes, how interesting. Heavy book!

Aristotle, now lemme see, yes I've heard of him.
I think. You know, I once knew this philosopher
chap, his name was Tony. Now this guy's philosophy was... Please, may I have my book back? I
don't mean to be unsociable, but I really am at a
very interesting chapter and would like to finish
it before I lose my train of thought. You can
tell me all about Tony later, all right? Why
don't you go and play some solitaire? Or listen
to the radio! Be a good boy now, won't you? Yes
m'am. Ah, well that takes care of that. Oh, I
wish there was something I could do around here,
as he listlessly takes a seat and ponders on
various entertainments. He can't think of any.
He gradually becomes a trifle gloomy.

When in comes HUBBY. The CHRISTMAS TREE is
ecstatic to see him back and quickly rushes over
to him with a profusion of hellos. Here lemme
take your coat. I got a million things to tell
you. I'll just put this coat away and I'll be
right back. Now don't go away.

HUBBY seems to be very tired and looks despondent.
Hello darling, how are you? A little kiss. Any
luck today my dear? No dear, I'm afraid not.
Couldn't find a job again. I don't know what I'm

going to do anymore. Oh don't give up, my dear,
something will turn up tomorrow. Don't be sad.
I'm sorry dear, but everything looks so hopeless.
You'll have better luck tomorrow, you'll see.
Yeah, tomorrow. Oh who am I kidding? WIFEY
becomes very sad when she sees HUBBY feeling so
defeated. HUBBY sees this and immediately repents
his earlier comments. Oh come dear, I didn't mean
that, I'm just very tired. Something's bound to
turn up soon, you're right. Oh well, I guess I
should have another look at these want ads.

HUBBY takes a seat and glumly goes through the
ads. WIFEY sadly returns to her book. Re-enter
the CHRISTMAS TREE to be greeted with this shroud
of gloom. Making an extra big effort to surmount
this contagious feeling, he cheerfully goes over
to HUBBY, pipe and slippers in hand and merrily
tries to fulfill his duties. Here you are, my
good sir, your pipe and your slippers. No you
just sit back and relax. Oh come now, don't read
this now, just relax a bit. Shall I get you a
drink? No? Well, no, put away the paper for a
while, a man's gotta rest sometime, right? All
work and no play, you know how the saying goes.
Here, lemme tell you a little story. The subject
came up a little while ago with the missus. Now
you see, I know this friend of mine who's a bit
of a philosopher, the chap's name's Tony, and so
anyway he claims that... Please, Mr Tree, I
appreciate what you're doing, but I really have
to look at these ads. I can't rest until I find
me a job. No, well you can glance at the oppor-
tunities column later, they won't run away. Oh
I think they will. Please Mr Tree, I need to be
left alone for a while. Don't get me wrong though,
I'd like to hear all about Tony, but we'll save it
for later, ok? Here why don't you look at the
sports section, here you are. Oh yes, the sports
section, thank you. All right, I'll...Sports!
I mean who cares? Sports! Oh well, I guess I
can't talk to him for a while. He's very upset.

I'd like to cheer him up but he won't let me.
And the missus don't feel like talking much either.
Why doesn't anyone want to talk to me? What's
with all this gloom? We should be having fun.
Fun...yeah! Oh well, they're just a little tired,
I guess. But that didn't stop them from being
cheerful a couple of days ago. They went along
with me then. They let me cheer them up, and they
enjoyed every minute of it too. Boy I was great
then. They laughed at all the jokes I told them.
Everything I did, they found funny. But they just
won't even let me try anymore. Am I getting in
the way perhaps? No, that's not possible. Only
a few days ago I was their wonderful tree, their
beautiful tree. No, people don't change so
suddenly. Or maybe I did something wrong? No,
that's not it either. I didn't do nothing wrong.
I guess they're just a little tired. Maybe I
should leave them alone for a while, 'til they get
over it.

Trying to come up with an explanation for the
couple's curious behavior, the CHRISTMAS TREE still
can't help feeling that he's somehow being left
out of the family. A little subdued now, he
quietly goes over to the window and disinterestedly
looks at the passersby. What he doesn't realize
is that he's gradually going through a transformation himself. This constant attempt at being
cheerful and the constant failure at sustaining
it is beginning to affect him. He begins to feel
very tired and irritable and listless. Being
happy doesn't come so easy anymore.

Music: The piano chord now commences. A single
moody chord repeated endlessly at a constant beat.

A lengthy pause.

Meanwhile, WIFEY quietly goes over to HUBBY and
tries to cheer him up a little. Don't worry, dear,
these are hard times, and there just aren't enough

jobs available. Something will turn up dear,
you'll see. And besides we have enough saved to
last us for another few weeks. We'll get by just
fine. And something's bound to turn up sooner or
later. Yes I suppose so, but I'd like us to be
able to afford a few... I have everything I want
dear. Yes, but I'd like us to go out more often,
I'd like us to get a decent place to live in,
some decent clothes, just look at the things we're
wearing, they're falling apart. Hush, dear, hush.
These things don't matter. But they do matter...
I love you, my sweet. I love you too, but...
Please. I'm sorry dear. A tender kiss. What
would I do without you?...They cuddle up tenderly,
still not quite able to shake off their melancholia,
but feeling a trifle more cheerful.

The CHRISTMAS TREE then turns around and notices
the two together. He brightens up as he looks on
fondly at the couple. He feels happy for them.
A little bit envious too, because he'd like so
much to be a part of the family, and he feels just
a little bit of a stranger. No that's silly, I'm
just misinterpreting this, I'm happy that they're
happy, and it shouldn't be any other way. My job
is only to see them content, whether it's me who
makes them so or whether they just happen to be
content without me having a hand in it, what does
it matter? But I can certainly make them a little
happier than they are. Yes I think this is a good
time to try one of my jokes on them. I've been
saving this one for a special occasion. Yup, I
think it's time for a biggie. Hello there. It's
nice to see the two of you smiling again. That's
the way it should always be, now am I right or
wrong? Yes, you're right Mr Christmas Tree. The
couple, feeling a little more sociable now, find
it easier to accomodate the CHRISTMAS TREE's
wishes. He is trying to be nice after all, and
he is very nice, but if only he didn't feel
obliged to keep it up all the time. He certainly
doesn't allow for any changes of mood, but he

means well, he means so well, the poor dear. The couple, knowing full well they both share these similar thoughts, give the CHRISTMAS TREE an encouraging smile.

Well what say you to a little story now? It's a very funny little story, I'm telling you. I've got laughs for this one every time and from all sorts of people. Feel game? Ok here goes. Well there was this plumber chap, see and there was this captain, from the navy, so one day... and the CHRISTMAS TREE gets himself deeply involved in his story,gesticulating and going through all the expressions of the characters. He feels himself cheering up as he gets deeper and deeper into the story. The couple sit attentively and listen to him with polite smiles, trying to get involved along with him.

The truth is the CHRISTMAS TREE's story isn't very funny, and although he relates it with gusto, and he tries real hard (boy does he try!), things somehow just don't come out very funny. The couple however continue smiling politely. And so the captain looks at the plumber and says, no thanks mister but your services won't be needed. Ha-Ha. Ha-Ha-Ha. The CHRISTMAS TREE is a little surprised at the lack of reaction. The captain actually says this to the man, that he doesn't need his services. Plumbing services. Get it?

The couple realize that was the punch-line, so they both force out some obliging guffaws. The CHRISTMAS TREE feels the laughs are false. You see the captain's ship was sinking all this time. Ha-Ha-Ha. Oh yes, of course, now I get it, ho-ho-ho, yes that's really funny. Yeah, I think it's pretty good, I got laughs for it all over the place. It's not a bad little story, right? Yes, oh yes, it's quite good. It's a really funny story. Yeah. The CHRISTMAS TREE knows they're

only trying to be polite. He hides his
embarrassment by being overly expansive. Yeah,
this jokes always been one of my reliables. Never
fails. Always does the trick. He feels very
embarrassed and lost all of a sudden, and the
couple's obliging politeness seems to make it
worse. The CHRISTMAS TREE tries to grope at
something, anything to save face. Putting on a
big smile, he does his Fred Astaire footwork. It
goes well, except for that last demanding step.
He's never had any trouble with it before, so it's
a surprise to everyone when he fumbles it. He
trips and almost falls.

The couple quickly rises to help. No, no, it's
all right, it's all right, I just tripped a little.
The CHRISTMAS TREE feels really terrible now.
HUBBY quickly tries to save him from further
embarrassment. It's that loose tile over there,
I must hammer it down, I should have done it last
week. WIFEY joins in too, knowing how bad the
CHRISTMAS TREE must feel, desperately trying to
find explanations. Yes, this place is so old,
everything's falling apart, I find myself trip-
ping all over the place.

The CHRISTMAS TREE, trying to be inconspicuous,
trying to hide his humiliation, and most painful
of all knowing that the couple knows exactly how
he feels, wishes they wouldn't offer him so much
sympathy. No, I... I... I guess I'm just getting
old, that's all. I feel a little tired today.
Guess I'm losing my touch. No, I'm out of practice, that's all. A bitter apology.

The couple can't bear to see the CHRISTMAS TREE
hurt himself so much, as he continues to make
stinging remarks about himself. Oh he makes to
laugh at them, tries to pass them off as jokes,
and the couple try to be good-natured about them
and laugh along with him. But they all know
better, as they feel their laughter souring up.

Let me get you a glass of water, all right? Yes
thanks, that'll be just fine. Just rest a little
Christmas Tree, here sit down, you're just a
little tired. Yeah, I'm a little tired, yeah,
thanks, thanks a lot. WIFEY returns with a glass
of water. Here, Christmas Tree, drink some water.
Yes, thank you, thank you very much. You feel all
right now? Yes, I feel much better, thank you.
Felt a little dizzy back there, don't know what
happened. Boy, that certainly shook me up. It's
the weather Christmas Tree, you've probably got a
cold or something. No, no, please don't worry,
I'm all right. No really, I feel just fine. Trying another attempt to perk up his spirits, the
CHRISTMAS TREE walks around feigning some boister-
ous haphazard imitations, Groucho Marx, Charles
Chaplin. The couple laugh appreciatively at his
efforts. Thank you, Christmas Tree, that was very
funny. You liked it huh, honest, I mean you
really...that was funny right? Yes Christmas Tree,
that was funny. See, I told you, all I need is
some practice, that's all. Hey, listen, have I
got a joke for you. Here sit down, I wanna tell
you this joke. Christmas Tree, perhaps you
should rest a little first? No, no, I feel fine,
I feel fine. Now are you ready for this? Hey,
you better fasten up your seat belts. All right,
Christmas Tree, but you musn't tire yourself...
Hush, hush, hush, hush, my story begins. All
right, now there was this blind guy and this deaf
chap, see. So one day they were walking along
when, and once again the CHRISTMAS TREE tries to
entertain the couple, for that was his job, and
that's what he was, an entertainer. His only
purpose in life was to plant that big smile on his
audience, and when he succeeded, boy, he was so
happy, he felt like he was in paradise. And this
time the CHRISTMAS TREE puts his all into the
joke. I've got to make them laugh with this one,
for he knows that if he fails with this joke, he's
finished.

And finished for good, because when an entertainer
loses his touch and fails to entertain any more,
then he's lost it for keeps. And that's something
you never get back. And so the CHRISTMAS TREE
fights for dear life. This isn't just an
ordinary joke any more, it's much, much more.
The CHRISTMAS TREE, gesturing and posing and
fighting and fighting, and so this blind guy
stops and says: speak louder boy, I can't hear
you.

The CHRISTMAS TREE stops and looks around,
searching for that smile. He looks despairingly
at the couple, almost pleading, just a little
laugh. Please. And the couple had made up their
minds to laugh heartily at his joke however
unfunny it turned out to be, if only to make the
CHRISTMAS TREE stop pitying himself so much. But
the CHRISTMAS TREE just blew that punch-line so
out of proportion, that the couple were sure there
would be more to the joke. They were caught by
surprise, unprepared for, they just didn't expect
the joke to finish so abruptly.

The couple finally realize the joke is over and
quickly start to laugh. Oh, that was so funny.
Oh yes, now I get it. Oh, ha ha, yes I see, yes
oh, that was hilarious.

The silence before the laughter, however, told
the CHRISTMAS TREE all he wanted to know. He
sees so clearly now. Oh, please don't, don't
laugh if you don't want to. No, don't, please,
no pity, no sympathy, you're only making it worse.
I've lost my touch, I know it, please stop
laughing. Thinking all these thoughts, the
humiliated CHRISTMAS TREE looks away, for he's
crying now and he can't control himself.

The couple feel there's something wrong. They
gradually ease out their laughter. Then they
stand, looking at each other, feeling really

awful, sensing the way the CHRISTMAS TREE is feeling. They fidget embarrassedly. What can we do?
HUBBY softly walks over to him and gently touches
him. That was a funny joke, Christmas Tree,
honest. The CHRISTMAS TREE tries to smile faintly.
He's unable to hide his tears. He tries to go off
to some corner, trying not to show his embarrassment, knowing he's unable to hide it. Don't look
at me, don't look at me, please. The couple try
to be sympathetic. WIFEY coming closer. I liked
that joke, Christmas Tree, honest. Yeah, o.k.,
thanks. HUBBY puts an arm on his shoulder, I
liked it too, really, I'm just feeling a little
tired, that's why I didn't get it at first. The
CHRISTMAS TREE, back turned to all, just wishes
they wouldn't feel so sorry for him, don't they
know it's not gonna make me feel any better. But
I liked the joke. O.k. thanks, so you liked the
joke, so fine. Fine, fine, fine. How many times
do you have to say it. This angry outburst from
the CHRISTMAS TREE catches the couple by surprise.
WIFEY sees the CHRISTMAS TREE crying and knows
that he didn't mean to be rude. Advancing:
Please Christmas Tree, why don't you rest... Why
don't you leave me alone. HUBBY, seeing how hurt
he is: I'm sorry, we're sorry, really, we didn't
mean to... Don't talk. Just don't talk if you're
only gonna lie. I'm finished. Why don't you say
that? Why don't you come out with the truth? You
ain't funny no more Christmas Tree. You just ain't
funny, you're a has been. Sobbing at every other
line, completely broken, humiliated, he tries to
strike out with the outraged vengeance of a once
proud man, desperately trying to hold on to his
self-respect, feeling it slip away, making things
worse and worse. I don't tell funny jokes any
more. Please, Christmas Tree, don't do that to
yourself, please. WIFEY pleads with him, in tears,
trying to understand him, trying to be sympathetic
and yet not pity him. Please Christmas Tree, stop
it, please, stop it, you're only making it worse
for all of us. Please. The CHRISTMAS TREE,

pitifully sinks down in his tears, trying to
apologize, I'm sorry. No, don't be. Please.
You're just tired. We all are. The CHRISTMAS
TREE subsides a little, then suddenly shivers
violently, feeling without mistake, feeling surely,
feeling it, and becoming very scared. The
comedian is dead.

Becoming almost maniacal, he tries to struggle up
from his knees. No, no, no, I'm not finished, I'm
not finished. I can still tell a joke. Here,
listen to this, this one's so funny... Please,
Christmas Tree don't... I wanna tell you a joke,
I wanna tell you this joke... Please... There
was this farmer once see and... and... and...

He stops half-way. He just stops and stares away
in the distance. He turns slightly and defeatedly
walks over to some corner. He's not crying any
more. He just stares into some distance with a
glassy-eyed stare. He seems to mumble a few
things to himself. He stops. He stops mumbling,
he stops staring. He smiles gently to the couple,
seeming to say, I'm all right now, please, I'd
like to be left alone for awhile.

The saddened couple feel the best thing to do is
leave him to himself for awhile and they slowly
go back to their seats and their reading material.
Of course, they don't read. Exchanging frequent,
worried glances with each other, they feign at
being immersed in their reading, their minds
being ever present with the CHRISTMAS TREE,
wanting to go up to him and comfort him, and yet
knowing that he wouldn't want to be pitied.

The CHRISTMAS TREE, sadly lost in his thoughts,
dries a tear. He has made up his mind. He
slowly removes his cap, places it aside. Removes
his vest and tie. Sadly puts them aside. Gives
them one last fond look, then turns away and
decides to leave.

The couple suddenly notice this and are scared
and stunned. They quickly get up and rush over
to him. No, what, what are you doing Christmas
Tree? Why have you removed your decorations?
Christmas Tree, no, please, stay here. WIFEY
gently implores, with moist eyes: Please
Christmas Tree, don't leave, don't leave us, we
love you very much. Please, stay, stay with us,
don't go.

No... I... I have to leave.

The CHRISTMAS TREE takes a step out when HUBBY
quickly holds him back. No please, we didn't
mean to, we're sorry. Please stay.

The CHRISTMAS TREE looks at them sadly. No, it's
not your fault, please don't think that. It's...
well... it's finished. I have to go.

The CHRISTMAS TREE silently goes to the door, and
looks back one last time. Thank you. He leaves.

HUBBY makes to go after him. WIFEY realizes it's
no use and holds him back.

He's right. It is finished. Christmas is over.

She sits down despondently and cries silently.
HUBBY sadly comes and sits beside her. He holds
her tightly. She holds on to him close.

They both look down sadly, holding on close to
each other.

SLOW BLACKOUT

Music fades out.

SCENE FIVE

Music: "Ave Maria"
Fading in as piano chord fades out.

The Wide Open.
Cold. Snow.

The CHRISTMAS TREE enters. Walking slowly,
dejectedly, hands in his pocket, he moves half-
heartedly. He takes a few steps forward and
stops, looking downcast at the ground. He
slowly turns around and stares for a long time at
the couple's little apartment. He then sadly
turns his back and slowly walks away from it,
towards the audience. He leans, standing,
against a wall, then slowly eases himself down
into a sitting position, legs stretched out,
trying to keep the cold away. He shudders.

Nice people. Nice couple. It was fun being with
them. Yes, it was real fun. I can still remember
that Christmas morning. Yeah, I can remember it
so clearly. Oh, how happy they were when they
saw their presents. And how pleased and touched,
when I gave them the crackers. And they insisted
I pull one of the crackers with them. Imagine,
me, a Christmas Tree. And we spent the whole of
Christmas together, we three, chatting and joking
and laughing and playing all sorts of games. And
What a wonderful dinner the missus had prepared.
Oh, we were so merry that day... so merry...

The CHRISTMAS TREE sadly looks in the direction
of the little apartment, thinking back on all the
fond memories of yesterweek. A tear rolls down
his cheek. He makes no attempt to hide it.

When slowly a little DOG wanders in. The DOG
perks up his ears as he notices the CHRISTMAS
TREE. He slowly takes a few steps forward, but

still keeps his distance. A stranger! You never know! He suspects the CHRISTMAS TREE of unfriend-liness. After all, what's he doing sitting out here, against a wall in the middle of the street in this kind of weather. No, thinks the DOG, I better be careful.

The CHRISTMAS TREE seeing the DOG, bravely smiles at him. He weakly stretches out his arm and beckons him to come closer.

The DOG doesn't know what to make of this. Should I? Shouldn't I? He's bewildered at this dilemma. Finally, he decides to play it safe and attempts a growl. Ruff! Being a small dog his growls don't sound like much, but he does his best to look mean. Don't try nothing funny with me boy 'cause I'm tough. Grrrr. I'm a mean son of a bitch, so you better watch out boy. Ruff, ruff. You just be careful boy. Grrrr.

He cautiously takes a step forward. The CHRISTMAS TREE is about to pat his head, but somehow the DOG didn't expect this sudden move-ment, so he acts on instinct and bites his hand. The CHRISTMAS TREE winces and merely looks at him sadly. Why? I only wanted to pat you.

The DOG immediately regrets what he did. Look, I, I'm sorry. I really am. Honest, I didn't mean to. Sorry. The DOG meekly tries to make up by licking the CHRISTMAS TREE'S hand, on the spot where he bit him. I'm sorry, Mister.

That's all right. Nice doggie. A moment of tender sympathy between the two, as the CHRISTMAS TREE gently pats the DOG'S head. The DOG showing his appreciation by putting on a friendly smile and making gentle contented sounds. The DOG can't help but feel the CHRISTMAS TREE'S sadness. He looks at him with deep sorrowful eyes. Come now, it's not as bad as all that. Oh nice,

doggie, my good friend, you wouldn't understand.
Oh, come on, nice sir, cheer up... won't you?

When suddenly a whistling call is heard from the
distance. His master! Oh, woeful dilemma! Oh,
nice, sir, I must go now, my master is calling
me. No, stay awhile longer, nice doggie, stay
and cheer me up a little. Just a little while.

I don't know, nice sir, I don't know, I'd like
to, but my master, he's calling...

The whistle again, more insistent.
I'm sorry... I must go. I'm sorry.
I understand.
Cheer up. Things aren't that bad.
I'll try.
Good-bye, nice sir.
Good-bye, nice doggie, good-bye my friend.

The helpless DOG reluctantly has to leave. Just
as he's about to exit, he turns to look once more
at the CHRISTMAS TREE, and exchanges one last
sympathetic smile. Poor fellow. The DOG sadly
hurries off to his master.

The CHRISTMAS TREE is now all alone.
It is bitterly cold out and he's shivering help-
lessly, but he can't feel the cold any more.
Once more he looks in the direction of the
couple's apartment... one last time.
He sadly turns away, letting the tears roll
freely down his cheeks.
With a heavy heart, crying silently, barely able
to move now for his whole body has become
painfully frozen, he feels his eyelids slowly
droop.

His eyes are shut now.

The tears seem to have stopped.

His head lolls unsteadily, slowly losing its
balance.

It seems to gradually drop lower... very slightly
... very gently... just a trifle uneven...

A sudden jerk forward.

The CHRISTMAS TREE dies.

SLOW BLACKOUT

Music ends.

THE END

CAST LISTS

MATHEMATICS was first presented at the Factory
Theatre Lab (Toronto), December 5, 1972. Music
by Mike Horwood. Directed by Hrant Alianak.

TANTRUMS was first presented at Theatre Passe
Muraille (Toronto), April 1972, with the
following cast: Nancy Oliver (LITTLE GIRL);
Neil Munro (PAPA, MAN in Tantrum Two, THOMAS);
Martha Gibson (MAMA, FEMALE USHER, WOMAN in
Tantrum Three); Alec Stockwell (SONNY, MALE
USHER, JAMES THE BUTLER, MAN in Tantrum Four);
Robert O'Ree (GASPARD, BISHOP); Milton Branton
(MAN in Tantrum Two, FREDERICK); Brenda Darling,
(WOMAN in Tantrum Two, CORA); Francine Volker
(WOMAN in Tantrum Two, DORA); Danny Griesdorf
(LITTLE BOY, JC); Jamey Preslar (VERA). Music
by Mike Horwood. Directed by Louis Del Grande.

CAST LISTS

BRANDY was first presented at Theatre Passe Muraille, May 1973, with the following cast: Robert O'Ree (JEREMIAH); Allan Aarons (HUBERT); Diana Knight (THE BLONDE); Anne-Marie Martin (THE BRUNETTE). Directed by Hrant Alianak.

WESTERN was first presented at Theatre Passe Muraille, September 1972, with the following cast: Allan Aarons (BART); Joan Cox (LILI); Patricia Conway (JEAN). Directed by Hrant Alianak.

CHRISTMAS was first presented at Theatre Passe Muraille, December 1973, with the following cast: Robert O'Ree (CHRISTMAS TREE); Bill Fleming (THE LUMBERJACK, THE DOG); Christopher Dobbs (YOUNG MAN); Eddie Benton (HIS WIFE); Edna Wolteger (THE VIOLINIST). Directed by Hrant Alianak.